Slice & Bake Cookies

SLICE & BAKE
COOKIES

FAST RECIPES FROM YOUR REFRIGERATOR OR FREEZER

Elinor Klivans *Photographs by* Yunhee Kim

CHRONICLE BOOKS

SAN FRANCISCO

As ever, thank you to Judith Weber, my agent, who is always in my corner.

The biggest thank-you to the brilliant and talented publishing team at Chronicle Books: Bill LeBlond, my editorial director, and Amy Treadwell, my editor, as well as Doug Ogan, Claire Fletcher, Alice Chau, Tera Killip, Peter Perez, and David Hawk, who made this book happen and are such a pleasure to work with; and to copy editor Jasmine Star, who understood my writing voice so well that she became my twin. Thanks also go to Yunhee Kim for her gorgeous photography.

I am grateful for my family of cookie bakers and happy cookie consumers: Laura and Michael Williams and Kate Steinheimer and Peter Klivans; Charlie, Oliver, and Miles; Madison, Max, Sadie, and Kip; and my father, who is proud of me and loves my cookies.

Thank you to those who tested my recipes so carefully: Jen Goldsmith, Melissa McDaniel, Kari McDonough, Rachel Ossakow, Dawn Ryan, Louise Shames, Kate Steinheimer, Laura Williams, and Oliver Williams.

A big thank-you to my circle of supporters and encouragers: Sue Chase, Michael Drons, Susan Dunning, Maureen Egan, Carole and Woody Emanuel, Rosalee and Chris Glass, Karen and Michael Good, Kat and Howard Grossman, Faith and David Hague, Helen and Reg Hall, Carolyn and Ted Hoffman, Kristine Kidd, Robert Laurence, Rosie Levitan, Gordon Paine, Joan and Graham Phaup, Pam and Stephen Ross, Louise and Erv Shames, Barbara and Max Steinheimer, Kathy Stiefel, Carol Witham, and Jeffrey Young.

Library of Congress Cataloging-in-Publication Data available.

ISBN 978-1-4521-0962-6

Manufactured in China

Design by Sarah Pulver
Typesetting by River Jukes-Hudson
Prop styling by Megan Hedgpeth
Food styling by Megan Schlow

The photographer wishes to thank designers Sarah Pulver and Alice Chau and the rest of the Chronicle team; my agents Pat Bates and Sandy Irani; and the amazing crew: prop stylist Megan Hedgpeth and her assistant Anne Eastman, food stylist Megan Schlow, and digital technician Adam McClure.

Grand Marnier is a registered trademark of Sociétédes Produits MARNIER-LAPOSTOLLE.
Hershey's chocolate is a registered trademark of the Hershey's Company.
Nutella is a registered trademark of Ferrero S.P.A.
Tabasco is a registered trademark of the McIlhenny Co.

10 9 8 7 6 5 4 3 2 1

Chronicle Books LLC
680 Second Street
San Francisco, California 94107
www.chroniclebooks.com

It is all about my family:
Laura, Michael, Charlie, Oliver,
and Miles; Kate, Peter,
Madison, Max, Sadie, and Kip;
and always for Jeff.

INTRODUCTION

Prepare to eat cookies, a lot of them, and anytime you want!

. . . .

I was in for a big surprise when I began testing recipes for this book. Although I've been baking cookies since I was a kid, I had no idea that the slice and bake technique could produce so many different kinds of cookies and so fast. I had no idea that any cookie dough (at least any I could think of) could be made using the slice and bake method. No more rolling and cutting out cookies for me. Now I produce cookies as fast as I can slice them. I am a speedy baker.

When I was developing recipes for this book, I made over 2,500 cookies. Some I sliced and baked as soon as the dough was cold and firm enough to slice. Some logs or slabs of dough I stacked in the freezer so they were ready to be freshly baked for any dinner party I gave, any dinner I attended, any of my neighbors, and any visit to friends or family, whether around the block or across the country. I shipped huge boxes of cookies to my children and grandchildren. My grandson, Oliver, learned quickly that if he called me and asked what I was doing,

I would invariably say I was baking cookies. Oliver would say, "Will you send me some?" Who could say no to that request?

I was surprised at how little room a dozen or so logs and slabs of dough took up in the freezer, and a dozen of them will make at least 360 cookies. When you do the math, it's clear what a great idea this is.

When I told people about the new cookbook I was writing, their reactions were interesting and so positive. The topic often brought up fond memories: "My grandmother always had a roll in the fridge." People who never baked were eager to try making these cookies: "Even I would buy this book and bake from it." I heard one remark repeatedly: "What a good idea." I agree. This is a classic "Why didn't I think of this idea before?" type of situation. I'm just happy that I finally did think of it. It is my very own cookie revolution, and in this revolution, all sides win.

INGREDIENTS, EQUIPMENT & TECHNIQUES

If there is one thing that all of these cookies have in common, it's that the ingredients and equipment are simple. You probably already have the majority of the ingredients in your pantry, and if you have several baking sheets and a saucepan, your equipment needs are mostly taken care of.

COOKIE INGREDIENTS

Good-quality ingredients are essential for making good cookies. Here are my preferences.

Butter, Oil, Cream Cheese & Sour Cream

Unsalted butter is used in all of the recipes requiring butter. I store it in my freezer to keep it fresh. Using unsalted butter allows you to control the exact amount of salt in the recipe. When using oil, I prefer corn or canola oil because they are low in saturated fat (the bad fat) and high in monounsaturated fat (the good fat). Both are tasteless and will not affect the flavor of cookies. Always smell oil before using it to make sure it's fresh and doesn't have a rancid or "off" odor. Use full-fat cream cheese and sour cream. Low-fat versions can affect the cookie dough and the baked cookies, and not in a good way.

Chocolate

Choose a good-quality chocolate that tastes good. The ingredients in white chocolate should include cocoa butter, and those in dark chocolate should include chocolate liquor or chocolate. Strange as it may seem, there are products made with artificial ingredients that give the impression of being chocolate.

Citrus Zest & Juice

Citrus zest is the rind of the fruit without any of the bitter white pith. Before grating zest from citrus fruit, wash the fruit with warm water and dry it. Be sure to grate the zest before squeezing any juice. Use fresh citrus juice in these recipes.

Eggs

Store eggs in the refrigerator and remember that cold eggs are easier to separate than those at room temperature. Leftover egg whites can be frozen for up to three months. Put them in a clean plastic freezer container and cover the container tightly. Label the container with the date and number of egg whites contained inside. Defrost the covered container of egg whites overnight in the refrigerator. Use egg yolks immediately or discard them.

Flour & Cornstarch

I tested the recipes using either unbleached all-purpose flour or cake flour. Cake flour contains less gluten than all-purpose flour and contributes to the tender texture of cookies. Store flour tightly covered, and keep it dry. Using cornstarch, which has no gluten, in place of some of the flour in shortbread cookie recipes makes for shortbread that is more tender.

Nuts

Nuts are harvested in the fall, so that's a good time to buy them. If stored in a tightly sealed freezer bag or airtight container, nuts can be kept in the freezer for as long as a year. Defrost frozen nuts before adding them to batters; if they're cold, this can affect the baking time and the final product.

Some of the recipes call for toasted nuts. To toast nuts, preheat the oven to 325°F/165°C/gas 3. Spread the nuts in a pan or on a baking sheet in a single layer and cook until fragrant and slightly darker in color. Toasting times are as follows: walnuts, pecans, and pine nuts, about 8 minutes; sliced or slivered blanched almonds, about 12 minutes, or until golden; and blanched whole almonds and skinned hazelnuts, about 15 minutes, or until golden. Cashews are typically sold roasted.

It's best to remove the bitter skin of hazelnuts (also known as filberts) before using them. The easiest solution, and what I recommend, is buying skinned hazelnuts. They are usually available at specialty markets. You can also purchase whole skinned hazelnuts and chopped toasted hazelnuts online from King Arthur Flour Company (www.kingarthurflour.com). Otherwise, I find blanching is the easiest way to remove hazelnut skins. To blanch them, fill a saucepan with enough water to cover the hazelnuts, then bring the water to a boil. Add the hazelnuts and boil them uncovered for 5 minutes. Drain the hazelnuts, then cover them with cold water for several minutes, until cool. Drain them again, then peel them with a small, sharp knife. They will dry out in the oven when they are toasted. If you won't be toasting them immediately, dry them with a clean dish towel and refrigerate or freeze them.

I prefer to chop nuts by hand, with a large, sharp knife, rather than in a food processor, as this allows more control over the size of the chopped pieces. When I list nuts as "finely chopped," I mean about 1/8 in/3 mm in size; by "coarsely chopped," I mean between 1/4 in/6 mm and 3/8 in/1 cm in size. For grinding nuts, a food processor fitted with the steel blade works well.

Salt, Baking Powder & Baking Soda

Kosher salt doesn't have additives, and that is the salt I use in all of my recipes. Note that if you substitute table salt, it's best to reduce the amount to about three-quarters or half. (Because table salt has finer crystals, it fills measuring spoons more fully.) Baking powder contains baking soda (which is alkaline), plus an acidic ingredient, and its leavening power is activated when it is combined with a liquid. Double-acting baking powders contain two acid ingredients, one activated by liquid and one activated by heat during baking. I use double-acting, aluminum-free baking powder. Store baking powder tightly covered, and don't use it after the expiration date on the can. Baking soda or sodium bicarbonate is an alkaline leavening that is activated when it is combined with an acid ingredient like sour cream, molasses, or buttermilk. If kept dry, baking soda can be stored indefinitely.

Spices & Extracts

Store spices in tightly covered containers and check that they are fresh by smelling and tasting them. As with chocolate, if a spice tastes good, it will add good flavor to cookies.

Always use pure vanilla extract, not imitation. The same goes for almond extract. Pure almond extract is a little more expensive, but its flavor is worth the additional cost.

TOOLS & EQUIPMENT FOR MAKING COOKIES

As mentioned, the equipment needed for making slice and bake cookies is very basic. It's likely that you already have everything you need. Here are a few recommendations.

Baking Sheets

All of the cookies in this book are baked on the same type of pan: baking sheets that measure about 17 in/43 cm long and 14 in/35.5 cm wide. Use heavy baking sheets with a shiny finish. The test for a heavy baking sheet is that you won't be able to bend it. Heavy aluminum baking sheets are a good choice. They have the advantage of being relatively light in weight, and their shiny finish deflects heat and helps prevent burned cookie bottoms. Plus, aluminum absorbs heat evenly, so your cookies will bake evenly. Rather than being rimmed along all four sides, baking sheets for cookies have curved rims at the ends or on one side for grasping the pan. This design allows cookies to slide off easily. Baking sheets with sides, usually 1 in/2.5 cm high (called jelly roll pans), work fine, but they hold fewer cookies and you can't slide the cookies off the sheet. For efficient baking, I recommend buying at least two, and preferably three, baking sheets.

Double Boiler

A double boiler is convenient for melting chocolate. You can also improvise with a heatproof bowl set over a saucepan of simmering water. Whether you use a double boiler or improvise, be sure the water in the bottom pan isn't in contact with the bowl or pot that contains the chocolate. If chocolate is overheated, it can "seize" and become grainy.

Electric Mixer

A handheld mixer is inexpensive and works well for most cookie doughs, but a stand mixer is a real workhorse and will keep your hands free during mixing.

Knives

You will need a large, sharp knife and a small serrated knife, such as a paring knife or tomato knife, for cutting the dough into slices.

Parchment Paper

I love parchment paper. When you use it, you can forget about greasing pans, forget about cookies sticking to the pan, and forget about washing pans. Just line baking sheets with parchment paper and you're good to go. Discard the paper after the cookies bake.

Utensils

It's useful to have two metal spatulas, one wide and one narrow. A narrow metal spatula comes in handy for spreading glazes and fillings on cookies. A wide metal spatula is essential for moving cookies around. Silicone spatulas are useful for scraping every bit of dough out of the mixing bowl. Accurate measuring is important, and I recommend that you have two sets of measuring spoons, one for dry ingredients and one for liquids, plus a set of dry measuring cups and two liquid measuring cups.

Wire Racks

All of the cookies in this book should be cooled on wire racks. If they remain on the hot baking sheet, they could over-bake or burn. Cooling on wire racks also allows air to circulate around the cookies; this is especially important in ensuring that crisp cookies have the intended texture. As with baking sheets, it's efficient to have at least two wire racks.

COOKIE MAKING & BAKING TECHNIQUES

MIXING THE COOKIE DOUGH

Most of the cookie doughs in this book are mixed following the same general procedure. Beat the butter and sugar to blend them until smooth, mix in any melted chocolate, and then add any eggs and liquid flavorings. Add the flour or flour mixture and any oatmeal, chocolate chips, fruit, dried fruit, or nuts. That's it. With some doughs, you might notice that adding cold eggs makes the batter looks curdled. This happens when cold eggs are combined with butter at room temperature. What you're actually seeing is small pieces of firm butter. Once the flour is added, the dough will look smooth again.

ASSESSING DONENESS

In my recipes I give several ways to determine whether cookies are baked. Color is one cue. Cookies might be done when the bottoms and edges are golden or when the centers are pale or golden. Another cue is the color of the bottom, which you can check by using a spatula to lift one cookie. That cookie might break, but accurately assessing doneness can save the whole batch. Plus, the baker gets to eat the broken cookies! The tops of chocolate cookies often change from shiny to dull as they near the end of their baking time. Another test is to lightly touch the center of a cookie to see if the center feels firm or soft.

Baking times are only a guideline. They must be approximate because so many factors can affect the amount of time needed. Ovens differ, the thickness of the cookies may differ, and the temperature of the dough might vary, from cold to room temperature. These all affect the time it takes cookies to bake. Cookies have short baking times, and these differences are measured in minutes. Follow the cues given in each recipe and check cookies often as the end of the baking time nears, and your cookies will turn out fine or, more likely, excellent.

SIMPLE DECORATIONS

Decorating cookies is fun, and it's a great activity to do with children. I spread newspaper on my kitchen floor to catch any spills, put out bowls of glazes and edible decorations (much of the latter is usually eaten before being applied to cookies). I have lots of plain baked cookies ready, such as Any-Holiday Sugar Cookies (page 40) or the cookies from Chocolate and Peppermint-Crunch Cookies (page 56). Creativity reigns, and when we're finished, I just roll up the newspaper, wipe the counter, and cleanup is done.

Some decorations can be added before cookies are baked. Nuts, sugar, or cinnamon sugar can be pressed onto the edges of logs of cookie dough or onto the sliced cookie dough. Chocolate chips and colored sugar can be pressed onto cookies before they bake. However, most decorations are added after cookies bake. Thick powdered sugar glazes, white or in colors, can be piped in a pattern onto cookies. Thin glazes can add shine or be used as glue to attach sprinkles, sugar decorations, small candies, small edible flowers, grated citrus zest, or chocolate shavings.

Dusting the tops of baked cookies with powdered sugar is one of the simplest methods of decoration. I like to take it a step further. Cut a thin strip of wax paper and use it to cover half a cookie or a band down the middle of a cookie, then dust the sugar over the cookie. When you remove the paper, the cookie will be half covered or have stripes of powdered sugar. This looks especially nice on the flat top of chocolate cookies or other dark-colored cookies.

Melted chocolate, in the form of coating (see pages 54 and 56) or ganache (see page 82) is a tasty decoration. Either can be drizzled over the top of cookies. Alternatively, half of the top of a cookie can be swept through either coating or ganache to coat it. White chocolate looks good on chocolate cookies and dark chocolate enhances vanilla or chocolate cookies. White chocolate can be made into a coating or ganache using the same methods as for milk chocolate and dark chocolate.

SERVING COOKIES

For many cookies there's nothing more to serving than lifting them off the baking sheet or out of a cookie jar. But you may sometimes want to arrange cookies, and I do have a few thoughts about that. Choose an assortment of cookies with different shapes, colors, and flavors. Use small platters that are no larger than 12 in/30.5 cm across. Large platters tend to look picked over when some of the cookies are gone. Small platters can be replenished often and look inviting. Arrange the same variety of cookie in a row, section, or circular pattern for an attractive presentation. Heaping cookies in baskets lined with colorful fabric or, for a fancier party, white linen napkins is another idea. The same ideas apply to savory cookies; however, it's best to keep each variety on its own plate or in its own basket so the flavors don't mingle.

STORING COOKIES

If properly packaged, most cookies can be stored perfectly for at least three days after baking. The best way to store cookies is to put them in a plastic container or tin with a tight seal, which protects them from both odors and humidity. Crisp cookies will retain their crisp texture if stored in a tin. It's a good idea to put a piece of wax paper between the layers of cookies, especially if the cookies have soft toppings.

Store each variety of cookie in its own container to prevent them from taking on other flavors. Most cookies can be stored at room temperature, but some frosted or filled cookies should be refrigerated. Each recipe specifies whether the baked cookies should be stored at room temperature or in the refrigerator.

FREEZING COOKIE DOUGH & BAKED COOKIES

Once shaped into logs, slabs, or other forms, cookie dough should be wrapped in plastic wrap and then aluminum foil to protect it in the freezer. Be sure to label each package with the date and its contents. Defrost it in the refrigerator and keep its wrapping on so any condensation forms on the wrapping, not the dough.

Many years ago, I made a great discovery about how to freeze baked cookies and have them taste just-baked, even after two months in the freezer: I wrap several cookies together in plastic wrap before storing them in an airtight container. It takes only a minute or two to wrap up a batch of cookies in these smaller parcels, and it make a big difference in their flavor and texture, sealing out air in a way that doesn't happen if they're just stacked in a container. Defrost the cookies in the container or wrapped in the plastic to prevent any condensation from forming on the cookies.

TRANSPORTING COOKIES

I'm a cookie courier. Whether I take my cookies around the block or ship them across an ocean, careful packaging is what gets them to their destination in good condition.

Most slice and bake cookies are good candidates for shipping. The only exceptions are those that have fillings or toppings, especially those made with chocolate, that might melt in warm temperatures; and those with fillings that require refrigeration. Cookies with fillings or toppings that might melt can be sent when the weather is cool.

When shipping cookies, it's important to use plenty of packing material and to double box all packages. Choose rigid plastic containers or tins large enough to hold the cookies. Then find a sturdy carton that will hold the cookie containers. Fill the bottom of the cookie containers with a layer of crumpled wax paper, then wrap the cookies in plastic wrap and stack them in the container. To prevent shifting, put a layer of wax paper between the layers of cookies. Fill any air space with crumpled wax paper and leave enough room to add about 1 in/2.5 cm of crumpled wax paper at the top. Fill the container but don't pack it tightly. Seal the container and tape the lid on to secure it. Wrap the container carefully in bubble wrap or a thick layer of paper (newspaper is fine).

To pack the carton, put a cushioning layer of crumpled newspaper or packing material, such as bubble wrap or packing peanuts, in the bottom. Put the cookie container or containers in the box and add crumpled newspaper or packing material around the containers so they won't shift in the carton. You now have a cushioned container inside a cushioned box. Seal the carton and rest assured that your cookies will travel safely.

When I carry cookies on an airplane or other public transport, I package them in a container as described for shipping, including taping the lid on securely, and put the container in my carry-on luggage.

SLICE & BAKE COOKIE KNOW-HOW

The dough for all of these cookies is quick and easy to mix, and forming the cookies is as simple as slicing the dough.

As I baked my way through the cookies while developing the recipes, I noticed that they have some common traits. My newfound knowledge helped me be more consistently successful in making the cookies better and making them more quickly. Here's what I learned:

- I found that almost any cookie dough can be formed into a shape and become a slice and bake cookie. If a dough is soft and sticky, chilling will firm it. The only exceptions I encountered were a foamy meringue preparation and a liquid lace cookie batter—cookies that aren't made from a dough.

- When rolling logs of dough, using the palms of your hands rather than your fingers will produce a smoother log. For square logs, rotate the dough and pat it on all four sides to make long flat sides and sharp edges. If the dough is sticky, shape it on plastic wrap (sticky dough will stick to wax paper).

- When a soft dough is formed into a log, it might flatten somewhat during chilling. Refrigerate the log just until it begins to firm up, then roll it back and forth until it has a uniform shape and return it to the refrigerator.

- Doughs that contain melted chocolate firm up quickly—as soon as the chocolate becomes cold. Butter is another ingredient that causes the dough to firm more quickly as it chills.

- Most of these recipes produce two logs or slabs of dough. One piece can be refrigerated and baked over several days and one can be frozen. If refrigerated, bake the cookies within three days. If you like, you can divide each piece of dough for baking smaller batches of cookies. If you do so, be aware that if a baking sheet isn't full, the cookies will probably bake more quickly.

- The best way to defrost dough is to put the wrapped dough in the refrigerator overnight. This assures that the dough will be evenly cold and won't have any frozen spots when you're ready to slice and bake it.

- When cold, dough slices evenly, whereas dough at room temperature squishes and loses its shape when cut, and frozen dough is either too hard to slice or may crumble when cut. One exception is the dough for Almond Macaroons (page 28), which must be cut when frozen.

- Generally, thick slices or pieces of dough produce chewy cookies, and thin ones produce crisp cookies.

- Cookies that are cut evenly and to the same size will be finished baking at the same time. I use a ruler to measure the first few slices and then try to cut the remaining cookies the same. I never get them exactly even, but I try to keep them as similar as I can. If some cookies are thinner or thicker than others, they may bake more quickly or slowly. You can always use a wide metal spatula to remove thinner cookies and let the rest bake longer.

- When slicing logs or long square pieces of dough, take care to cut straight down. After cutting several slices, there's a tendency to cut at an angle and produce slices with an uneven thickness. (I speak from experience here.) This will make a cookie that is thinner on one side. This isn't a problem with slabs of dough.

- For dough that includes hard pieces (such as chocolate chips), if it cracks or a piece breaks off or crumbles during slicing or cutting, put the cookie on the baking sheet and press the pieces together. I form this kind of dough into slabs and usually don't have a problem with cracking.

- Yields may vary a bit, especially depending on the size of the cut cookies. However, knowing the approximate yield will help you make cookies of about the same size and serves as an indication of the number you can expect to have.

- Any of these doughs can be frozen before baking, and all of the cookies can be frozen after they're baked (see page 15).

CHEWY COOKIES

Soft centers and crisp edges—that's what makes a chewy cookie, and what makes them so appealing. These are the folksy, cookie jar classics, such as oatmeal-raisin cookies, chocolate chip cookies, and molasses cookies.

Certain ingredients and dough attributes contribute to making a cookie chewy. Generally, soft dough makes for a soft cookie and firm dough makes for a crisp one. Some of the doughs in this section are quite sticky, and when first mixed will make oddly shaped logs. The solution is to shape them in plastic wrap as best you can, then refrigerate for 15 to 30 minutes. Once chilled, the dough will be firmer, and you can roll it again, still in its plastic wrap.

Fresh and dried fruits and ground nuts add to the texture of chewy cookies. Several of the cookies in this section have chunks of chocolate or regular-size chocolate chips in the dough. If these doughs are formed into a log and sliced, the hard chocolate will make the slices crumble. So this type of cookie dough is patted into a slab and cut into squares. This helps prevent crumbling, and the soft dough miraculously spreads into rounds during baking. Mini chocolate chips don't cause crumbling when the dough is sliced.

SUGAR & SPICE *snickerdoodles*

MAKES **36**

Snickerdoodles hail from the Midwest, but the entire United States has adopted these beloved cookies, which are chewy in the middle and, thanks to a cinnamon sugar coating, very crisp on the outside.

MEASURING & MIXING TIME *10 minutes*

BAKE AT *350°F/180°C/gas 4* FOR ABOUT *13 minutes*

2 ½ cups/315 g unbleached all-purpose flour

2 tsp cream of tartar

1 tsp baking soda

¼ tsp salt

1 ½ cups/300 g sugar

2 tsp ground cinnamon

1 cup/225 g unsalted butter, at room temperature

2 eggs

1 ½ tsp vanilla extract

Sift the flour, cream of tartar, baking soda, and salt into a medium bowl. Set aside.

In a small bowl, stir ¼ cup/50 g of the sugar and the cinnamon together until evenly blended. Set aside.

Put the butter and the remaining 1¼ cups/250 g of sugar in the bowl of an electric mixer and beat on medium speed until smoothly blended, about 1 minute. Stop the mixer and scrape the sides of the bowl as needed. Mix in the eggs and vanilla until blended, about 1 minute. Reduce the speed to low, add the flour mixture, and mix just until incorporated.

Divide the dough into two equal parts. Put each on a large piece of plastic wrap and form into a roughly shaped log 9 in/23 cm long and 1½ in/4 cm in diameter. Sprinkle 1 tbsp of the cinnamon sugar over each log and roll back and forth to form a smooth, evenly coated cylinder. Wrap in the plastic wrap. Reserve the remaining cinnamon sugar. Refrigerate for at least 3 hours or overnight, until firm, or wrap aluminum foil over the plastic wrap and freeze for up to 2 months.

Frozen dough will be difficult to cut and should be defrosted in the refrigerator for at least 3 hours or overnight first.

When ready to bake the cookies, position a rack in the middle of the oven. Preheat the oven to 350°F/180°C/gas 4. Line two baking sheets with parchment paper.

Use a large, sharp knife to cut each cold log into 18 slices about ½ in/12 mm thick. Place the cookies 3 in/7.5 cm apart on the baking sheets. Sprinkle each with about ¼ tsp of the reserved cinnamon sugar.

Bake the cookies one sheet at a time just until the edges and bottoms are light brown but the centers remain pale, about 13 minutes.

Let cool on the baking sheet for 10 minutes. Use a wide metal spatula to transfer the cookies to a wire rack to cool completely.

The cookies can be stored in a tightly covered container at room temperature for up to 3 days.

OLD-FASHIONED OATMEAL-RAISIN *cookies*

MAKES 24

Some cookies are perennial favorites, and oatmeal-raisin cookies are at the top of that list. I'm not one to challenge a classic, but I did want my cookies to include a generous quantity of raisins and plenty of oatmeal for crunch (plus, this sneaks in a bit of extra nutrition).

MEASURING & MIXING TIME *10 minutes*

BAKE AT *350°F/180°C/gas 4* FOR ABOUT *15 minutes*

1 ¼ cups/155 g unbleached all-purpose flour

¾ tsp baking soda

¼ tsp salt

1 ½ tsp ground cinnamon

½ cup/115 g unsalted butter, at room temperature

¾ cup/150 g firmly packed dark brown sugar

¼ cup/50 g granulated sugar

1 egg

1 ½ tsp vanilla extract

1 ½ cups/125 g old-fashioned rolled oats

1 ½ cups/255 g seedless raisins

Sift the flour, baking soda, salt, and cinnamon into a medium bowl. Set aside.

Put the butter, brown sugar, and granulated sugar in the bowl of an electric mixer and beat on medium speed until smoothly blended, about 1 minute. Stop the mixer and scrape the sides of the bowl as needed. Mix in the egg and vanilla until blended, about 1 minute. Reduce the speed to low, add the flour mixture and rolled oats, and mix just until incorporated. Add the raisins and mix just until evenly distributed.

Divide the dough into two equal parts. Put each on a large piece of plastic wrap and form into a log 6 in/15 cm long and 1¾ in/4.5 cm in diameter. Roll each back and forth to form a smooth cylinder, then wrap in the plastic wrap. Refrigerate for at least 3 hours or overnight, until firm, or wrap aluminum foil over the plastic wrap and freeze for up to 2 months.

Frozen dough will be difficult to cut and should be defrosted in the refrigerator for at least 3 hours or overnight first.

When ready to bake the cookies, position a rack in the middle of the oven. Preheat the oven to 350°F/180°C/gas 4. Line two baking sheets with parchment paper.

Use a large, sharp knife to cut each cold log into 12 slices about ½ in/12 mm thick. Place the cookies 2 in/5 cm apart on the baking sheets.

Bake the cookies one sheet at a time just until the edges are firm but the centers feel soft if touched lightly, about 15 minutes.

Let cool on the baking sheet for 10 minutes. Use a wide metal spatula to transfer the cookies to a wire rack to cool completely.

The cookies can be stored in a tightly covered container at room temperature for up to 3 days.

CHOCOLATE CHUNK *cookies*

Only the edges of these soft and chewy cookies are crisp. Cutting the chocolate into chunks of assorted sizes causes them to melt into delicious and irregular-shaped blobs of chocolate scattered throughout every cookie. Chocolate chips, on the other hand, keep their uniform shape after baking. Forming this dough into slabs makes it easy to cut the dough into cookies without any cracking due to the larger chunks.

MEASURING & MIXING TIME *10 minutes*

BAKE AT *350°F/180°C/gas 4* FOR ABOUT *13 minutes*

1 ¼ cups/155 g unbleached all-purpose flour

1 tsp baking soda

¼ tsp salt

½ cup/115 g unsalted butter, at room temperature

¾ cup/150 g firmly packed light brown sugar

2 tbsp granulated sugar

1 egg

1 tsp vanilla extract

12 oz/340 g semisweet chocolate, cut into ¼-in/6-mm to
     ½-in/12-mm pieces

Sift the flour, baking soda, and salt into a medium bowl. Set aside.

Put the butter, brown sugar, and granulated sugar in the bowl of an electric mixer and beat on medium speed until smoothly blended, about 1 minute. Stop the mixer and scrape the sides of the bowl as needed. Mix in the egg and vanilla until blended, about 1 minute. Reduce the speed to low, add the flour mixture, and mix just until incorporated.

Add the chocolate and mix just until evenly distributed.

Divide the dough into two equal parts. Put each on a large piece of plastic wrap and pat into a square slab 5 in/12 cm across. Wrap each slab in the plastic wrap. Refrigerate for at least 3 hours or overnight, until firm, or wrap aluminum foil over the plastic wrap and freeze for up to 2 months.

Frozen dough will be difficult to cut and should be defrosted in the refrigerator for at least 3 hours or overnight first.

When ready to bake the cookies, position a rack in the middle of the oven. Preheat the oven to 350°F/180°C/gas 4. Line two baking sheets with parchment paper.

Use a large, sharp knife to cut each chilled slab into 9 pieces, cutting three rows across and three rows down (like a tic-tac-toe pattern). Although the cookies are cut into squares, they will spread into rounds during baking. Place the cookies 3 in/ 7.5 cm apart on the baking sheets.

Bake the cookies one sheet at a time just until the edges are firm but the centers feel soft if touched lightly, about 13 minutes.

Let cool on the baking sheet for 10 minutes. Use a wide metal spatula to transfer the cookies to a wire rack to cool completely.

The cookies can be stored in a tightly covered container at room temperature for up to 3 days.

GINGER, GINGER *cookies*

If you like spicy ginger cookies that are crisp on the outside and chewy on the inside and have the added zip of crystallized ginger pieces, this recipe is for you. If you like spicy ginger cookies that are crisp all the way through, this recipe is also for you—just bake the cookies two or three more minutes. Measure the oil in a measuring cup, then measure the molasses in the same cup. That way the molasses won't stick to the measuring cup.

MEASURING & MIXING TIME *10 minutes*

BAKE AT *350°F/180°C/gas 4* FOR ABOUT *10 minutes*

2 cups/255 g unbleached all-purpose flour

2 tsp baking soda

¼ tsp salt

1 tsp ground cinnamon

1 tsp ground ginger

½ tsp ground cloves

¼ tsp ground nutmeg

½ cup/120 ml canola or corn oil

¼ cup/60 ml molasses

1 cup/200 g firmly packed dark brown sugar

1 egg

4 tbsp granulated sugar

½ cup/115 g crystallized ginger, chopped

Sift the flour, baking soda, salt, cinnamon, ginger, cloves, and nutmeg into a medium bowl. Set aside.

Put the oil, molasses, brown sugar, and egg in the bowl of an electric mixer and beat on medium speed until smoothly blended, about 30 seconds. Stop the mixer and scrape the sides of the bowl as needed. Reduce the speed to low, add the flour mixture, and mix just until incorporated.

Divide the dough into two equal parts. Put each on a large piece of plastic wrap and form into a roughly shaped

log 12 in/30.5 cm long and 1 in/2.5 cm in diameter. Sprinkle 1 tbsp of the granulated sugar over each log and roll back and forth until evenly coated. Then sprinkle half of the ginger over each log and roll back and forth until evenly coated. Refrigerate for about 30 minutes, then roll each log again to form a more uniformly shaped cylinder. Refrigerate for at least 2½ hours or overnight, until firm, or wrap aluminum foil over the plastic wrap and freeze for up to 2 months.

Frozen dough will be difficult to cut and should be defrosted in the refrigerator for at least 3 hours or overnight first.

When ready to bake the cookies, position a rack in the middle of the oven. Preheat the oven to 350°F/180°C/gas 4. Line two baking sheets with parchment paper.

Use a large, sharp knife to cut each cold log into 12 slices about 1 in/2.5 cm thick. Place the cookies 3 in/7.5 cm apart on the baking sheets. Sprinkle each with about ¼ tsp of the remaining granulated sugar.

Bake the cookies one sheet at a time just until they flatten and the tops form several cracks, about 10 minutes.

Let cool on the baking sheet for 10 minutes. Use a wide metal spatula to transfer the cookies to a wire rack to cool completely.

The cookies can be stored in a tightly covered container at room temperature for up to 3 days.

VERY SPICY *joe froggers*

MAKES **20**

When my friend Becky Brace found out I was writing this book, she said that her grandmother always had a roll of cookie dough in the refrigerator. Then she sent me her family's traditional New England recipe for these old-fashioned molasses cookies, which truly are known as Joe Froggers. Originally, Joe Froggers were served by Aunt Crese and Old Black Joe Brown, who ran a tavern in Marblehead, Massachusetts, after the Revolutionary War. These are large, dark, chewy cookies that are just right for enjoying beside a fire on a blustery winter night.

MEASURING & MIXING TIME **10 minutes**

BAKE AT **350°F/180°C/gas 4** FOR ABOUT **13 minutes**

COOKIES
2 cups/255 g unbleached all-purpose flour
¾ tsp salt
1 tsp ground ginger
½ tsp ground cloves
¼ tsp ground nutmeg
¼ tsp ground allspice
⅔ cup/160 ml molasses
3 tbsp water
¾ tsp baking soda
1 tbsp dark rum
6 tbsp/85 g unsalted butter, at room temperature
½ cup/100 g sugar

DRIZZLE (optional)
⅔ cup/70 g powdered sugar
1 tbsp plus up to 2 tsp hot water
1 tsp corn syrup
½ tsp vanilla extract

Make the cookies. Sift the flour, salt, ginger, cloves, nutmeg, and allspice into a medium bowl. Set aside.

In a medium bowl, gently stir the molasses, water, and baking soda together until evenly blended. Stir in the rum.

Put the butter and sugar in the bowl of an electric mixer and beat on medium speed until smoothly blended, about 1 minute. Stop the mixer and scrape the sides of the bowl as needed. Reduce the speed to low and add the flour mixture in three additions alternating with the molasses mixture in two additions, beginning and ending with the flour mixture and mixing just until the flour is incorporated and a smooth dough forms.

Divide the dough into two equal parts. Put each on a large piece of plastic wrap and form into a roughly shaped log 8 in/20 cm long and 1½ in/4 cm in diameter. Roll each back and forth to form a smooth cylinder, then wrap in the plastic wrap. Refrigerate for about 1 hour, then roll each log again to form a more uniformly shaped cylinder. Refrigerate for at least 2 hours or overnight, until firm, or wrap aluminum foil over the plastic wrap and freeze for up to 2 months.

Frozen dough will be difficult to cut and should be defrosted in the refrigerator for at least 3 hours or overnight first.

When ready to bake the cookies, position a rack in the middle of the oven. Preheat the oven to 350°F/180°C/gas 4. Line two baking sheets with parchment paper.

Use a large, sharp knife to cut each cold log into 10 slices a generous ¾ in/2 cm thick. Place the cookies 2 in/5 cm apart on the baking sheets.

Bake the cookies one sheet at a time just until the edges are firm but the centers feel soft if touched lightly, about 13 minutes.

Let cool on the baking sheet for 10 minutes. Use a wide metal spatula to transfer the cookies to a wire rack to cool completely.

Make the drizzle, if desired. In a medium bowl, stir the powdered sugar, 1 tbsp of the hot water, and the corn syrup and vanilla together to make a thick but smooth and pourable glaze, adding more hot water as needed, 1 tsp at a time, to reach the desired consistency.

Use a small spoon to drizzle the glaze over the cookies. Let the glaze set at room temperature.

The cookies can be stored between layers of wax paper in a tightly covered container at room temperature for up to 3 days.

ALMOND *macaroons*

With their almond paste, almond extract, and sliced almonds, there is no doubt what these cookies are about. The cookie itself is chewy, but the sliced almond topping adds a bit of crunch. Since there is no flour in these macaroons, they are gluten-free. Almond paste is sold in 8-oz/225-g cans and 7-oz/200-g plastic tubes. Either quantity works fine for these cookies. The dough is very soft even when frozen and should be sliced when frozen. The sliced almonds will toast as the cookies bake.

MEASURING & MIXING TIME *10 minutes*

BAKE AT *350°F/180°C/gas 4* FOR ABOUT *18 minutes*

7 to 8 oz/200 to 225 g almond paste, broken into pieces
3 tbsp unsalted butter, at room temperature
⅓ cup/65 g sugar
1 egg white
½ tsp vanilla extract
½ tsp almond extract
1 tbsp cornstarch
1 cup/115 g sliced raw almonds

Put the almond paste and butter in the bowl of an electric mixer and mix on low speed until smoothly blended, about 2 minutes. Stop the mixer and scrape the sides of the bowl as needed. Mix in the sugar until blended, about 20 seconds. Mix in the egg white, vanilla, and almond extract until blended, about 1 minute. Add the cornstarch and mix just until incorporated.

Divide the dough into two equal parts. Put each on a large piece of plastic wrap and form into a log 5½ in/14 cm long and 1¼ in/3 cm in diameter. Roll each back and forth to form a smooth cylinder, then wrap in the plastic wrap. Twist the ends of the plastic wrap tightly and secure with string or twist ties to hold this soft dough in its smooth log shape.

Wrap aluminum foil over the plastic wrap and freeze at least overnight or for up to 2 months. This frozen dough is soft enough to cut and should not be defrosted before it is sliced.

When ready to bake the cookies, position a rack in the middle of the oven. Preheat the oven to 350°F/180°C/gas 4. Line two baking sheets with parchment paper.

Remove one log of dough from the freezer. Spread the sliced almonds on a large piece of plastic wrap. Unwrap the log and roll it in the sliced almonds, gently pressing the nuts into the dough. Don't try to press half of the almonds into each log; the remaining almonds are sprinkled over the tops of the cookies before baking.

Use a large, sharp knife to cut the frozen log into 16 slices about ⅓ in/8 mm thick. The dough will be soft and easy to cut. Place the cookies 1½ in/4 cm apart on the baking sheets. Sprinkle each cookie with sliced almonds. Repeat with the remaining log of dough.

Bake the cookies one sheet at a time until the edges begin to brown, about 18 minutes.

Let cool on the baking sheet for 10 minutes. Use a wide metal spatula to transfer the cookies to a wire rack to cool completely.

The cookies can be stored in a tightly covered container at room temperature for up to 3 days.

ESPRESSO & DARK CHOCOLATE *chipsters*

MAKES 32

As a longtime fan of chocolate chip cookies, I spend no small part of my life figuring out ways to make variations (so I can eat more of them). My latest success is this cookie, in which one recipe of dough is divided in half, and then one part is flavored with espresso and the other with cocoa powder. As they cool, these cookies sink and form ripples on top. This indicates that the cookies will be soft and chewy.

MEASURING & MIXING TIME *10 minutes*

BAKE AT *350°F/180°C/gas 4* FOR ABOUT *14 minutes*

1 ¼ cups/155 g unbleached all-purpose flour

½ tsp baking soda

½ tsp salt

½ cup/115 g unsalted butter, at room temperature

½ cup/100 g firmly packed light brown sugar

6 tbsp/75 g granulated sugar

1 egg

1 tsp vanilla extract

2 tbsp unsweetened Dutch-process cocoa powder, sifted

2 cups/340 g semisweet chocolate chips

1 ½ tsp instant espresso powder

1 tbsp water

Sift the flour, baking soda, and salt into a medium bowl. Set aside.

Put the butter, brown sugar, and granulated sugar in the bowl of an electric mixer and beat on medium speed until smoothly blended, about 1 minute. Stop the mixer and scrape the sides of the bowl as needed. Mix in the egg and vanilla until blended, about 1 minute. Reduce the speed to low, add the flour mixture, and mix just until incorporated.

Transfer half of the dough to a medium bowl and set aside. Using the electric mixer on low speed, add the cocoa powder to the remaining dough and mix just until incorporated. Add 1 cup/170 g of the chocolate chips and mix just until evenly distributed. Set aside.

Dissolve the espresso in the water, then add it to the dough in the medium bowl and stir with a large spoon just until incorporated. Add the remaining 1 cup/170 g of chocolate chips and stir just until evenly distributed. You will have a bowl of chocolate dough and a bowl of coffee-flavored dough.

Divide the chocolate dough into two equal parts. Put each on a large piece of plastic wrap and form into a log 8½ in/ 21.5 cm long and 1½ in/4 cm in diameter. Divide the coffee dough into two equal parts and form each into a log the same size as the chocolate logs. Using a small spoon or your fingers, press a slight indentation along the length of each chocolate log. If the dough is sticky, lightly flour the spoon or your fingers. Press a coffee log onto each chocolate log to form two double-colored logs. Roll each back and forth to form a smooth cylinder, then wrap in the plastic wrap. Refrigerate for at least 3 hours or overnight, until firm, or wrap aluminum foil over the plastic wrap and freeze for up to 2 months.

Frozen dough will be difficult to cut and should be defrosted in the refrigerator for at least 3 hours or overnight first.

When ready to bake the cookies, position a rack in the middle of the oven. Preheat the oven to 350°F/180°C/gas 4. Line two baking sheets with parchment paper.

Use a large, sharp knife and a sawing motion (this helps cut through the chocolate chips) to cut each log into 16 slices a generous ½ in/12mm thick. Place the cookies 2 in/5 cm apart on the baking sheets. If any slices crumble, press them back together.

Bake the cookies one sheet at a time just until the edges are firm but the centers feel soft if touched lightly, about 14 minutes.

Let cool on the baking sheet for 10 minutes. Use a wide metal spatula to transfer the cookies to a wire rack to cool completely.

The cookies can be stored in a tightly covered container at room temperature for up to 3 days.

IN THE CHIPS
toffee, butterscotch & chocolate chip cookies

These cookies are loaded with good stuff—butterscotch chips, toffee, and chocolate chips—and the recipe makes large cookies. Because the slices are so thick, they are easy to cut despite the large quantity of chips. The toffee melts and caramelizes during baking, which may cause the cookies to stick to the parchment paper. It's a good idea to butter the parchment paper so the cookies release easily.

MEASURING & MIXING TIME *10 minutes*

BAKE AT *350°F/180°C/gas 4* FOR ABOUT *13 minutes*

2 cups/255 g unbleached all-purpose flour

½ tsp baking soda

¼ tsp salt

1 tsp instant coffee granules

1 tbsp water

¾ cup/170 g unsalted butter, at room temperature

½ cup/100 g firmly packed light brown sugar

¼ cup/50 g granulated sugar

2 eggs

1 tsp vanilla extract

1 ½ cups/255 g semisweet chocolate chips

1 cup/170 g butterscotch chips

4 oz/115 g toffee candy (such as Skor), coarsely crunched

Sift the flour, baking soda, and salt into a medium bowl. Set aside.

Dissolve the coffee granules in the water. Put the butter, brown sugar, and granulated sugar in the bowl of an electric mixer and beat on medium speed until smoothly blended, about 1 minute. Stop the mixer and scrape the sides of the bowl as needed. Mix in the eggs, vanilla, and dissolved coffee until blended, about 1 minute. Reduce the speed to low, add the flour mixture, and mix just until incorporated. Add the

chocolate chips, butterscotch chips, and toffee and mix just until evenly distributed.

Divide the dough into two equal parts. Put each on a large piece of plastic wrap and form into a log 11 in/28 cm long and 1¾ in/4.5 cm in diameter. Roll each back and forth to form a smooth cylinder, then wrap in the plastic wrap. Refrigerate for at least 3 hours or overnight, until firm, or wrap aluminum foil over the plastic wrap and freeze for up to 2 months.

Frozen dough will be difficult to cut and should be defrosted in the refrigerator for at least 3 hours or overnight first.

When ready to bake the cookies, position a rack in the middle of the oven. Preheat the oven to 350°F/180°C/gas 4. Line two or three baking sheets with parchment paper. Butter the paper.

Use a large, sharp knife to cut each cold log into 14 slices a generous ¾ in/2 cm thick. Place the cookies 3 in/7.5 cm apart on the baking sheets.

Bake the cookies one sheet at a time just until the tops are a light golden color, about 13 minutes.

Let cool on the baking sheet for 15 minutes. Use a wide metal spatula to transfer the cookies to a wire rack to cool completely.

The cookies can be stored between layers of wax paper in a tightly covered container at room temperature for up to 3 days.

WALNUT BROWNIE *cookies*

All of the fudge of a brownie, all of the ease of making brownies, and all of the speed of a slice and bake cookie. The logs of dough are rolled in chopped walnuts that become toasted and quite crunchy during baking. Mini chocolate chips melt and disappear into the cookies during baking, adding to the fudge brownie texture. Before chilling this dough is sticky, but as the butter and chocolate become cold, the dough quickly firms up.

MEASURING & MIXING TIME *10 minutes*

BAKE AT *350°F/180°C/gas 4* FOR ABOUT *13 minutes*

2 oz/55 g unsweetened chocolate, chopped

8 oz/225 g semisweet chocolate, chopped

½ cup plus 2 tbsp/145 g unsalted butter, cut into pieces

1¼ cups/155 g unbleached all-purpose flour

½ tsp baking powder

½ tsp salt

2 eggs

1¼ cups/250 g granulated sugar

1 tsp vanilla extract

1⅓ cups/225 g miniature semisweet chocolate chips

1 cup/115 g walnuts, coarsely chopped

Put both chocolates and the butter in a heatproof bowl or the top of a double boiler and place it over a saucepan of barely simmering water or the bottom of the double boiler; the water should not touch the bowl. Stir until the chocolates and butter are melted and smooth. Set aside for 15 minutes to cool and thicken slightly.

Sift the flour, baking powder, and salt together in a medium bowl. Set aside.

Put the eggs, sugar, and vanilla in the bowl of an electric mixer and beat on medium speed until fluffy and slightly lightened in color, about 1 minute. Stop the mixer and scrape the sides of the bowl as needed. Reduce the speed to low, add the chocolate mixture, and mix just until incorporated. Add the flour mixture and mix just until no white streaks remain. Add the chocolate chips and mix just until evenly distributed.

Divide the dough into two equal parts. Put each on a large piece of plastic wrap and form into a roughly shaped log 7½ in/19 cm long and 1½ in/4 cm in diameter, then wrap in the plastic wrap. Refrigerate for about 15 minutes (this dough firms quickly), then roll each log again to form a more uniformly shaped cylinder. Unwrap and sprinkle half of the walnuts over each log and roll back and forth until evenly coated, gently pressing the nuts into the dough. Rewrap in the plastic wrap. Refrigerate for at least 2½ hours or overnight, until firm, or wrap aluminum foil over the plastic wrap and freeze for up to 2 months.

Frozen dough will be difficult to cut and should be defrosted in the refrigerator for at least 3 hours or overnight first.
continued...

WALNUT BROWNIE *cookies (continued)*

When ready to bake the cookies, position a rack in the middle of the oven. Preheat the oven to 350°F/180°C/gas 4. Line two or three baking sheets with parchment paper.

Use a large, sharp knife to cut each cold log into 15 slices about ½ in/12 mm thick. If any slices crumble, press them back together. Place the cookies 2 in/5 cm apart on the baking sheets.

Bake the cookies one sheet at a time until the tops crackle and feel firm on the surface but still soft inside if touched lightly and a toothpick inserted in the center comes out with sticky batter clinging to it, about 13 minutes.

Let cool on the baking sheet for 10 minutes. Use a wide metal spatula to transfer the cookies to a wire rack to cool completely. Serve warm or at room temperature.

The cookies can be stored in a tightly covered container at room temperature for up to 2 days.

CHOICES

Omit the walnuts. The cookies will spread about ½ in/12 mm wider, but the baking time remains the same.

CHOCOLATE *fudgies*

MAKES **16**

Four chocolates, thickly sliced dough, and a short baking time are the secret to achieving the soft, fudgy texture of these cookies. If desired, dust with powdered sugar when cool.

MEASURING & MIXING TIME **15 minutes**

BAKE AT **350°F/180°C/gas 4** FOR ABOUT **11 minutes**

1 oz/30 g unsweetened chocolate, chopped

4 oz/115 g semisweet chocolate, chopped

1¼ cups/155 g unbleached all-purpose flour

2 tbsp unsweetened Dutch-process cocoa powder

1 tsp cream of tartar

½ tsp baking soda

¼ tsp salt

½ tsp instant coffee granules

1 tsp water

½ cup/115 g unsalted butter, at room temperature

½ cup/100 g firmly packed light brown sugar

¼ cup/50 g granulated sugar

1 egg

1 tsp vanilla extract

1 cup/170 g miniature semisweet chocolate chips

Put both chocolates in a heatproof bowl and place it over a saucepan of barely simmering water; the water should not touch the bowl. Stir until the chocolates are melted and smooth. Set aside for about 5 minutes to cool slightly.

Sift the flour, cocoa powder, cream of tartar, baking soda, and salt into a medium bowl. Set aside.

Dissolve the coffee granules in the water. Put the butter, brown sugar, and granulated sugar in the bowl of an electric mixer and beat on medium speed until smoothly blended, about 1 minute. Add the melted chocolate and mix just until

incorporated. Stop the mixer and scrape the sides of the bowl as needed. Mix in the egg, vanilla, and dissolved coffee until blended, about 30 seconds. Reduce the speed to low, add the flour mixture, and mix just until incorporated. Add the chocolate chips and mix just until evenly distributed.

Divide the dough into two equal parts. Put each on a large piece of plastic wrap and form into a roughly shaped log 8 in/20 cm long and 1½ in/4 cm in diameter. Roll each back and forth to form a smooth cylinder, then wrap in the plastic wrap. Refrigerate for about 30 minutes, then roll each log again to form a more uniformly shaped cylinder. Refrigerate for at least 1½ hours or overnight, until firm. Or wrap aluminum foil over the plastic wrap and freeze for up to 2 months. Frozen dough will be difficult to cut and should be defrosted in the refrigerator for at least 3 hours or overnight first.

When ready to bake the cookies, position a rack in the middle of the oven. Preheat the oven to 350°F/180°C/gas 4. Line two baking sheets with parchment paper.

Use a large, sharp knife to cut each cold log into 8 slices about 1 in/2.5 cm thick. Place the cookies 3 in/7.5 cm apart on the baking sheets.

Bake the cookies one sheet at a time just until they feel firm on the surface but still soft if touched lightly. The cookies should bake no longer than 11 minutes.

Let cool on the baking sheet for 10 minutes. Use a wide metal spatula to transfer the cookies to a wire rack to cool completely.

The cookies can be stored in a tightly covered container at room temperature for up to 3 days.

CRISP COOKIES

Maybe it is the crumbs that fall or the crunch as you bite into a crisp cookie, but there is no doubt that these cookies are one of life's pleasures. Crisp cookies come in such a wide variety. There are the many flavors of buttery shortbread, crisp chocolate wafers, tiny chocolate chip cookies, flaky cinnamon cookies, or coconut-crusted thumbprints, to name just a few.

The shapes of crisp cookies can push the boundaries. Small rectangular cookies can be pinched in the center to form butterfly shapes, and shortbread can be shaped and cut into squares, rectangles, rounds, or triangles. Different colors of dough can be rolled up together and sliced to create multicolored spirals. Multicolored dough can be stacked and sliced into striped cookies and slabs of dough can be cut into batons.

As varied as these cookies are, they are all fast to put together and bake quickly. So dive in and be ready to let the crumbs fall where they will.

ANY-HOLIDAY SUGAR *cookies*

These are ideal cookies for celebrating every holiday. They are a butter-sugar cookie with a smooth top that makes a perfect palette for decorating. Two easy decorating options are either sprinkling the cookies with colored or plain sugar, or adding a simple glaze. Let your imagination have free rein and have fun decorating. I've given lots of decorating and flavoring ideas on the facing page, but anything goes as long as it's edible. From Valentine's Day to Halloween to, of course, the winter holidays, this is very merry cookie baking. Of course, the cookies are fine left plain and served as a butter cookie.

MEASURING & MIXING TIME **10 minutes**

BAKE AT **350°F/180°C/gas 4** FOR ABOUT **17 minutes**

COOKIES

1 cup/225 g unsalted butter, at room temperature

1 cup/200 g granulated sugar

¼ tsp salt

1 egg yolk

2 tsp vanilla extract

½ tsp almond extract

2 ¼ cups/285 g unbleached all-purpose flour

---

2 tbsp granulated sugar, or 3 tbsp colored sugar for sprinkling (optional)

GLAZE (optional)

1 ¼ cups/125 g powdered sugar

2 tbsp plus 1 to 2 tsp milk, cream, or fresh lemon juice

Make the cookies. Put the butter, sugar, and salt in the bowl of an electric mixer and beat on medium speed until smoothly blended, about 2 minutes. Stop the mixer and scrape the sides of the bowl as needed. Mix in the egg yolk, vanilla, and almond extract until blended, about 1 minute.

Reduce the speed to low, add the flour, and mix just until a smooth dough forms and starts to come away from the sides of the bowl, about 1 minute.

Divide the dough into two equal parts. Put each on a large piece of plastic wrap and form into a log 6 in/15 cm long and 1¾ in/4.5 cm in diameter. Roll each back and forth to form a smooth cylinder, then wrap in the plastic wrap. Refrigerate for at least 3 hours or overnight, until firm, or wrap aluminum foil over the plastic wrap and freeze for up to 2 months.

Frozen dough will be difficult to cut and should be defrosted in the refrigerator for at least 3 hours or overnight first.

When ready to bake the cookies, position a rack in the middle of the oven. Preheat the oven to 350°F/180°C/gas 4. Line two or three baking sheets with parchment paper.

Use a large, sharp knife to cut each cold log into 24 slices about ¼ in/6 mm thick. Place the cookies 2 in/5 cm apart on the baking sheets. Sprinkle each cookie with granulated or colored sugar, if desired, lightly pressing the sugar onto the cookies.

Bake the cookies one sheet at a time until the edges begin to brown but the centers remain pale, about 17 minutes.

Let cool on the baking sheet for 10 minutes. Use a wide metal spatula to transfer the cookies to a wire rack to cool completely.

Make the glaze, if desired. In a medium bowl, stir the powdered sugar and 2 tbsp of the milk together to form a thin, smooth glaze, adding a bit more milk as needed to achieve the desired consistency. A thicker consistency acts as a simple frosting and a thinner consistency adds shine or acts as "glue" for holding other decorations.

Use a narrow metal spatula to spread a thin layer of glaze over the top of each cookie. Let the glaze set at room temperature. If using the glaze with other decorations, see the suggestions below.

Whether plain or decorated, the cookies can be stored in a tightly covered container at room temperature for up to 3 days. After the tops of any decorated cookies are firm, layer them in the container between sheets of wax paper to protect them.

DECORATING IDEAS

Make the optional glaze, adjusting the amount of liquid as needed to yield a syrupy consistency. Spread the glaze evenly over the cookies to help sprinkles, coconut, nuts, or seasonal sugar decorations to adhere to the top of cookies.

Melt chocolate, let it firm slightly, and then use small cookie cutters to cut out shapes. Attach them to the cookies with a bit of glaze.

Pipe a glaze that has a thick consistency onto the cookies in stripes, other patterns, or shapes, such as trees or half moons. If you sprinkle on a topping, it will stick to the glaze to form the same pattern or shape.

Make additional glaze, divide the glaze into smaller portions, and use food coloring to color each portion differently. You can use toothpicks or small spoons to swirl and marbleize colors.

For a spiderweb pattern, spread a thick layer of glaze on a cookie. Then, with a contrasting color of glaze, use a toothpick to draw two thin circles, one inside the other, and spoon a small drop in the center. Using a toothpick and beginning at the center, drag the tip back and forth through the circles to form a web pattern.

For a feathered pattern, spread a thick layer of glaze on a cookie. Then, with a contrasting color of glaze, use a toothpick to draw three or four straight lines across the cookie. Then drag the toothpick across the lines, alternating directions to form a feather pattern.

Melt some chocolate (see page 56) and sweep the tops of the cookies through it to half cover the tops. Or melt dark and white chocolate separately and dip one side of the cookies in the dark chocolate and one side in the white chocolate. Dip the first side in white chocolate, then put the cookies on a wire rack to let the coating firm up. Dip the other side in dark chocolate and, again, put the cookies on a wire

rack to let the chocolate firm up. Another option is to dip one side of a cookie and drizzle melted chocolate on the other side.

Like glaze, melted chocolate can be used to help attach other decorations, such as shaved chocolate or chocolate curls.

Above all, have fun!

SQUARED-OFF LEMON *shortbread*

MAKES **36**

The Scots are famous for making good shortbread, and these cookies use their traditional mixing method. The dry ingredients are mixed with cold butter pieces until buttery crumbs form. When the vanilla and fresh lemon juice are added, the dough forms large clumps that hold together.

MEASURING & MIXING TIME *10 minutes*

BAKE AT *325°F/165°C/gas 3* FOR ABOUT *25 minutes*

---

1 ½ cups/185 g unbleached all-purpose flour

¾ cup/85 g cornstarch

¼ cup/50 g granulated sugar

¼ cup/25 g powdered sugar, plus more for dusting

¼ tsp salt

1 cup/225 g cold unsalted butter, cut into 32 pieces

1 ½ tsp grated lemon zest

1 tbsp fresh lemon juice

1 tsp vanilla extract

Sift the flour, cornstarch, granulated sugar, powdered sugar, and salt into the bowl of an electric mixer and mix on low speed for about 15 seconds to combine the ingredients. Add half of the butter pieces and the lemon zest and mix until buttery crumbs begin to form, about 2 minutes. Stop the mixer and scrape the sides of the bowl as needed. Add the remaining butter pieces and mix until no loose flour remains, about 1 minute. Add the lemon juice and vanilla and mix until the dough holds together in large clumps, about 45 seconds.

Divide the dough into two equal parts. Put each on a large piece of plastic wrap and form into a square log 4½ in/11 cm long and 1½ in/4 cm square at the ends. Wrap in the plastic wrap and rotate the wrapped dough, patting it on all four sides to form long, straight, even edges. Refrigerate for at

least 3 hours or overnight, until firm, or wrap aluminum foil over the plastic wrap and freeze for up to 2 months.

Frozen dough will be difficult to cut and should be defrosted in the refrigerator for at least 3 hours or overnight first.

When ready to bake the cookies, position a rack in the middle of the oven. Preheat the oven to 325°F/165°C/gas 3. Line two baking sheets with parchment paper.

Use a large, sharp knife to cut each cold log into 18 slices about ¼ in/6 mm thick. Place the cookies 1 in/2.5 cm apart on the baking sheets. (These cookies don't spread much.)

Bake the cookies one sheet at a time until the tops feel firm if touched lightly and the edges begin to brown, about 25 minutes.

Let cool on the baking sheet for 10 minutes. Use a wide metal spatula to transfer the cookies to a wire rack to cool completely. Dust lightly with powdered sugar.

The cookies can be stored in a tightly covered container at room temperature for up to 3 days.

CHOICES

Drizzle the cookies with a glaze made from powdered sugar and lemon juice. Stir enough lemon juice into 1 cup/100 g of powdered sugar to make a thin, syrupy glaze.

OATMEAL SHORTBREAD *batons*

MAKES 56

Butter and brown sugar are paired up in this crisp and crunchy oatmeal shortbread, making for a heavenly aroma as they bake. Be sure to use rolled oats that are labeled "old-fashioned" rather than "quick-cooking."

MEASURING & MIXING TIME *10 minutes*

BAKE AT *350°F/180°C/gas 4* FOR ABOUT *20 minutes*

1 cup/125 g unbleached all-purpose flour

3 tbsp cornstarch

½ tsp salt

1 tsp ground cinnamon

¾ cup/170 g unsalted butter, at room temperature

½ cup/100 g firmly packed light brown sugar

1 tsp vanilla extract

¾ cup/60 g old-fashioned rolled oats

Sift the flour, cornstarch, salt, and cinnamon into a medium bowl. Set aside.

Put the butter, brown sugar, and vanilla in the bowl of an electric mixer and beat on medium speed until smoothly blended, about 1 minute. Stop the mixer and scrape the sides of the bowl as needed. Reduce the speed to low, add the flour mixture, and mix just until the dough holds together in large clumps, about 45 seconds. Add the oats and mix just until evenly distributed.

Divide the dough into 2 equal parts. Put each on a large piece of plastic wrap and pat into a rectangular slab 4 in/ 10 cm long, 3½ in/9 cm wide, and about 1 in/2.5 cm thick. Wrap each in the plastic wrap. Refrigerate for at least 3 hours or overnight, until firm, or wrap aluminum foil over the plastic wrap and freeze for up to 2 months.

Frozen dough will be difficult to cut and should be defrosted in the refrigerator for at least 3 hours or overnight first.

When ready to bake the cookies, position a rack in the middle of the oven. Preheat the oven to 350°F/180°C/gas 4. Line two baking sheets with parchment paper.

Use a large, sharp knife to cut each cold slab in half crosswise to make two strips 3½ in/9 cm long and 2 in/5 cm wide. Cut each half crosswise into 14 slices about ¼ in/6 mm thick. Each slab yields 28 pieces about 2 in/5 cm long and 1 in/2.5 cm wide. Place the cookies 1 in/2.5 cm apart on the baking sheets. (These cookies don't spread much.)

Bake the cookies one sheet at a time until the edges are light brown, about 20 minutes.

Let cool on the baking sheet for 10 minutes. Use a wide metal spatula to transfer the cookies to a wire rack to cool completely.

The cookies can be stored in a tightly covered container at room temperature for up to 3 days.

BUTTER-PECAN *bow ties*

These nutty, powdered sugar–coated cookies include both ground and chopped pecans and literally melt in your mouth. The dough is first cut into thin rectangular shapes, and then each is pinched in the center to scrunch the dough together and form a bow tie shape. However, the cookies can also be left as simple rectangles. The dough is sliced ¼ in/6 mm thick. If cut any thinner, the cookies will have a tendency to break.

MEASURING & MIXING TIME *10 minutes*

BAKE AT *325°F/165°C/gas 3* FOR ABOUT *20 minutes*

1 cup/125 g unbleached all-purpose flour

½ tsp baking powder

¼ tsp salt

½ cup/115 g unsalted butter, at room temperature

¼ cup/25 g powdered sugar, plus more for dusting

¾ tsp ground cinnamon

1 tsp vanilla extract

½ cup/55 g pecans, finely ground

¼ cup/30 g pecans, coarsely chopped

Sift the flour, baking powder, and salt into a medium bowl. Set aside.

Put the butter, powdered sugar, cinnamon, and vanilla in the bowl of an electric mixer and beat on medium speed until smoothly blended, about 1 minute. Stop the mixer and scrape the sides of the bowl as needed. Decrease the speed to low, add the flour mixture, and mix just until incorporated. Add the ground and chopped pecans and mix just until evenly distributed.

Divide the dough into two equal parts. Put each on a large piece of plastic wrap and pat into a rectangular slab about 5 in/12 cm long, 2½ in/6 cm wide, and about 1 in/2.5 cm

thick. Wrap each in the plastic wrap. Refrigerate for at least 3 hours or overnight, until firm, or wrap aluminum foil over the plastic wrap and freeze for up to 2 months.

Frozen dough will be difficult to cut and should be defrosted in the refrigerator for at least 3 hours or overnight first.

When ready to bake the cookies, position a rack in the middle of the oven. Preheat the oven to 325°F/165°C/gas 3. Line two baking sheets with parchment paper.

Remove one piece of dough from the refrigerator. Using a sharp knife and a sawing motion, cut the cold slab crosswise into 20 slices about ¼ in/6 mm thick and 2½ in/6 cm long. Place the cookies 1 in/2.5 cm apart on the baking sheets. (These cookies don't spread much.) Gently pinch the center of each strip to form a bow tie shape. Repeat with the second slab of dough.

Bake the cookies one sheet at a time until the edges are light brown, about 20 minutes.

Let cool on the baking sheet for 10 minutes. Use a wide metal spatula to transfer the cookies to a wire rack to cool completely. Dust lightly with powdered sugar.

The cookies can be stored between layers of wax paper in a tightly covered container at room temperature for up to 3 days.

GRANDMOTHER SOPHIE'S BUTTER *cookies*

I only know my grandmother Sophie through photographs, but I think of her and her baking legacy whenever I make these cookies, and that is often. My mom used to put a chocolate chip in the middle of each, and I sometimes press half a pecan onto the top. One year, for Halloween I used food coloring to make them orange (not my proudest cookie). With or without these additions, they remain the most meltingly tender and buttery cookies I've ever eaten.

MEASURING & MIXING TIME *10 minutes*

BAKE AT *350°F/180°C/gas 4* FOR ABOUT *20 minutes*

1 cup/225 g unsalted butter, at room temperature

¼ tsp salt

⅔ cup/130 g sugar

2 egg yolks

1 tsp vanilla extract

¼ tsp almond extract

2 cups/255 g unbleached all-purpose flour

42 chocolate chips (optional)

42 pecan halves (optional)

Put the butter and salt in the bowl of an electric mixer and beat on medium speed just until blended, about 15 seconds. Beat in the sugar until smoothly blended, about 1 minute. Stop the mixer and scrape the sides of the bowl as needed. Mix in the egg yolks, vanilla, and almond extract until blended, about 1 minute. Reduce the speed to low, add the flour, and mix just until incorporated.

Divide the dough into two equal parts. Put each on a large piece of plastic wrap and form into a log 7 in/17 cm long and 1½ in/4 cm in diameter. Roll each back and forth to form a smooth cylinder, then wrap in the plastic wrap. Refrigerate for at least 3 hours or overnight, until firm, or wrap aluminum foil over the plastic wrap and freeze for up to 2 months.

Frozen dough will be difficult to cut and should be defrosted in the refrigerator for at least 3 hours or overnight first.

When ready to bake the cookies, position a rack in the middle of the oven. Preheat the oven to 350°F/180°C/gas 4. Line two baking sheets with parchment paper.

Use a large, sharp knife to cut each cold log into 21 slices about ⅓ in/8 mm thick. Place the cookies 1½ in/4 cm apart on the baking sheets. Press a chocolate chip, flat-side up, or a pecan half in the center of each cookie, if desired.

Bake the cookies one sheet at a time until the edges are lightly browned, about 20 minutes.

Let cool on the baking sheet for 10 minutes. Use a wide metal spatula to transfer the cookies to a wire rack to cool completely.

The cookies can be stored in a tightly covered container at room temperature for up to 3 days.

CHOICES

- *Add 1 tsp of grated lemon or orange zest to the cookie dough.*
- *Sprinkle colored sugar or chopped nuts over the cookies before baking them.*
- *Melt some chocolate (see page 56) and drizzle it over the baked cookies.*

CHOCOLATE-DIPPED BUTTER *nuggets*

MAKES **72**

This recipe makes three slabs of dough that are cut into rectangular cookies. The slabs can be used one at a time, which leaves a nice stash in the freezer just waiting to be baked. Once baked, the ends of the cookies are dipped in a simple chocolate coating. Before the chocolate coating firms up, it can be dipped in chopped nuts or crushed peppermint candy.

MEASURING & MIXING TIME **10 minutes**

BAKE AT **325°F/165°C/gas 3** FOR ABOUT **18 minutes**

COOKIES

1 cup/125 g unbleached all-purpose flour

6 tbsp/40 g cornstarch

½ tsp baking powder

¼ tsp salt

1 cup/225 g unsalted butter, at room temperature

⅔ cup/130 g sugar

2 egg yolks

1 tsp vanilla extract

SEMISWEET CHOCOLATE COATING

9 oz/255 g semisweet chocolate, chopped

2 tbsp canola or corn oil

Make the cookies. Sift the flour, cornstarch, baking powder, and salt into a medium bowl. Set aside.

Put the butter and sugar in the bowl of an electric mixer and beat on medium speed until smoothly blended, about 1 minute. Stop the mixer and scrape the sides of the bowl as needed. Mix in the egg yolks and vanilla until blended, about 1 minute. Reduce the speed to low, add the flour mixture, and mix just until incorporated.

Divide the dough into three equal parts. Put each on a large piece of plastic wrap and form into a rectangular slab 6 in/15 cm long, 3 in/7.5 cm wide, and about ¾ in/2 cm thick. Wrap in the plastic wrap. Refrigerate for at least 3 hours or overnight, until firm, or wrap aluminum foil over the plastic wrap and freeze for up to 2 months.

Frozen dough will be difficult to cut and should be defrosted in the refrigerator for at least 3 hours or overnight first.

When ready to bake the cookies, position a rack in the middle of the oven. Preheat the oven to 325°F/165°C/gas 3. Line two baking sheets with parchment paper.

Use a large, sharp knife to cut each cold slab in half lengthwise to make two strips that are 6 in/15 cm long and 1½ in/4 cm wide. Cut each half crosswise into 12 slices about ½ in/12 mm thick. Each slab yields 24 pieces about 1½ in/4 cm long and ½ in/12 mm wide. Place the cookies 1 in/2.5 cm apart on the prepared baking sheets. (These cookies don't spread much.)

Bake the cookies one sheet at a time until the edges begin to brown, about 18 minutes.

Let cool on the baking sheet for 10 minutes. Use a wide metal spatula to transfer the cookies to a wire rack to cool completely. ***continued…***

CHOCOLATE-DIPPED BUTTER *nuggets (continued)*

Make the coating. Put the chocolate and oil in a heatproof bowl or the top of a double boiler and place it over a saucepan of barely simmering water or the bottom of the double boiler; the water should not touch the bowl. Stir until the chocolate is melted and smooth. Scrape the mixture into a medium bowl and set aside for about 5 minutes to cool and thicken slightly.

Spread out a large piece of wax paper. Dip the ends of each cookie in the chocolate coating, covering about one-third of the cookie altogether. Place the cookies on the wax paper and let sit until the chocolate coating is firm, about 1 hour at room temperature, or sooner if refrigerated. You will have some chocolate coating left over for another use, but the larger quantity makes it easier to dip the cookies.

The cookies can be stored between layers of wax paper in a tightly covered container at room temperature for up to 3 days. If the kitchen temperature is warm, store them in the refrigerator to keep the chocolate firm.

CHOICES

- *The dough can be flavored with 1½ tsp of grated lemon or orange zest.*
- *After dipping the ends of the cookies in chocolate, dip them in chopped nuts. Pecans, walnuts, toasted hazelnuts, or toasted almonds work well.*
- *After dipping the ends of the cookies in chocolate, dip them in crushed peppermint hard candy.*

STRAWBERRY & TOASTED COCONUT *thumbprints*

My mom used to make these buttery cookies that have a bright center of strawberry jam. Sometimes my mom would roll the dough in chopped nuts and put seedless raspberry or apricot jam in the center.

MEASURING & MIXING TIME *10 minutes*

BAKE AT *300°F/150°C/gas 2* FOR ABOUT *35 minutes*

1 cup/125 g unbleached all-purpose flour

¼ tsp baking powder

⅛ tsp salt

½ cup/115 g unsalted butter, at room temperature

¼ cup/50 g sugar

1 egg, separated

1 tsp grated orange zest

1 tbsp fresh orange juice

1 tsp vanilla extract

¼ tsp almond extract

1 cup/95 g sweetened shredded dried coconut

2 tbsp strawberry jam

Sift the flour, baking powder, and salt together in a small bowl. Set aside.

Put the butter and sugar in the bowl of an electric mixer and beat on medium speed until smoothly blended, about 1 minute. Stop the mixer and scrape the sides of the bowl as needed. Mix in the egg yolk, orange zest, orange juice, vanilla, and almond extract until blended, about 1 minute. Reduce the speed to low, add the flour mixture, and mix just until incorporated.

Divide the dough into two equal parts. Put each on a large piece of plastic wrap and form into a log 6 in/15 cm long and 1 in/2.5 cm in diameter. Roll each into a smooth cylinder.

Use a fork to beat the egg white until foamy. Use a pastry brush to lightly coat each roll with egg white. Sprinkle half of the coconut over each log and roll back and forth until evenly coated, gently pressing the coconut into the dough. Wrap in the plastic wrap. Refrigerate for at least 3 hours or overnight, until firm, or wrap aluminum foil over the plastic wrap and freeze for up to 2 months.

Frozen dough will be difficult to cut and should be defrosted in the refrigerator for at least 3 hours or overnight first.

When ready to bake the cookies, position a rack in the middle of the oven. Preheat the oven to 300°F/150°C/gas 2. Line a baking sheet with parchment paper.

Use a large, sharp knife to cut each cold log into 12 slices about ½ in/12 mm thick. Place the cookies 1 in/2.5 cm apart on the baking sheets. (These cookies don't spread much.) Use a small spoon or your thumb to press an indentation, about ¼ in/6 mm deep, in the center of each cookie. Put about ¼ tsp of jam in each indentation.

Bake the cookies just until the tops feel firm if touched lightly and the cookies are lightly browned, about 35 minutes.

Let cool on the baking sheet for 10 minutes. Use a wide metal spatula to transfer the cookies to a wire rack to cool completely.

The cookies can be stored between layers of wax paper in a tightly covered container at room temperature for up to 3 days.

TINY, CRISP CHOCOLATE CHIP *cookies*

It takes more than one of these cookies to make a serving. Happily, the recipe makes a lot of them—108 to be exact. The thin cookies, which are loaded with mini chocolate chips, bake to round disks that are about 2 in/5 cm in diameter. Baking time is only about ten minutes, and these small cookies can darken quickly, so watch carefully to avoid burning.

MEASURING & MIXING TIME *10 minutes*

BAKE AT *350°F/180°C/gas 4* FOR ABOUT *10 minutes*

1 cup/125 g unbleached all-purpose flour

¾ tsp baking soda

⅛ tsp salt

¼ tsp ground cinnamon

6 tbsp/85 g unsalted butter, at room temperature

½ cup/100 g firmly packed light brown sugar

¼ cup/50 g granulated sugar

1 egg

1 tsp vanilla extract

1 cup/170 g miniature semisweet chocolate chips

Sift the flour, baking soda, salt, and cinnamon into a medium bowl. Set aside.

Put the butter, brown sugar, and granulated sugar in the bowl of an electric mixer and beat on medium speed until smoothly blended, about 1 minute. Stop the mixer and scrape the sides of the bowl as needed. Mix in the egg and vanilla until blended, about 1 minute. Reduce the speed to low, add the flour mixture, and mix just until incorporated. Add the chocolate chips and mix just until evenly distributed.

Divide the dough into two equal parts. Put each on a large piece of plastic wrap and form into a log 9 in/23 cm long and 1 in/2.5 cm in diameter. Roll each back and forth to form a smooth cylinder, then wrap in the plastic wrap. Refrigerate for at least 2 hours or overnight, until firm, or wrap aluminum foil over the plastic wrap and freeze for up to 2 months.

Frozen dough will be difficult to cut and should be defrosted in the refrigerator for at least 3 hours or overnight first.

When ready to bake the cookies, position a rack in the middle of the oven. Preheat the oven to 350°F/180°C/gas 4. Line two or three baking sheets with parchment paper.

Use a large, sharp knife to cut each cold log into 27 slices about ⅓ in/8 mm thick, then cut each slice in half. Each log will yield 54 cookies. The shape isn't important, as the cookies miraculously spread into neat rounds during baking. Place the cookies 1 in/2.5 cm apart on the baking sheets. (These cookies don't spread much.)

Bake the cookies one sheet at a time just until the cookies are evenly lightly browned, about 10 minutes.

Let cool on the baking sheet for 10 minutes. Use a wide metal spatula to transfer the cookies to a wire rack to cool completely.

The cookies can be stored in a tightly covered container at room temperature for up to 4 days.

SWEET & SALTED CHOCOLATE *cookies*

MAKES 24

Please don't pass these cookies by. At first glance they may look like simple chocolate cookies with a slightly crackled top. What they actually are is dark chocolate cookies with an intense flavor and an unusual (and good) crumbly texture. They're dotted with small pieces of chocolate and have a salty-sweet flavor. Add to all of that how easy they are to prepare, and you have a cookie worth making—often.

MEASURING & MIXING TIME *10 minutes*

BAKE AT *350°F/180°C/gas 4* FOR ABOUT *20 minutes*

1 cup/125 g unbleached all-purpose flour

¼ cup/30 g cake flour

⅓ cup/30 g unsweetened Dutch-process cocoa powder

½ tsp baking soda

¼ tsp salt

¾ cup/170 g unsalted butter, at room temperature

1 cup/200 g granulated sugar

1 egg yolk

1 tsp vanilla extract

⅓ cup/55 g miniature semisweet chocolate chips

Sea salt for sprinkling

Sift the all-purpose flour, cake flour, cocoa powder, baking soda, and salt into a medium bowl. Set aside.

Put the butter and sugar in the bowl of an electric mixer and beat on medium speed until lightened in color and fluffy, about 3 minutes. (This lengthier beating time is important for producing the crumbly texture of the cookies.) Stop the mixer and scrape the sides of the bowl as needed. Reduce the speed to low and mix in the egg yolk and vanilla until blended, about 30 seconds. Add the flour mixture and mix just until incorporated. Add the chocolate chips and mix just until evenly distributed.

Divide the dough into two equal parts. Put each on a large piece of plastic wrap and form into a log 6 in/15 cm long and 1½ in/4 cm in diameter. Roll each back and forth to form a smooth cylinder, then wrap in the plastic wrap. Refrigerate for at least 3 hours or overnight, until firm, or wrap aluminum foil over the plastic wrap and freeze for up to 2 months.

Frozen dough will be difficult to cut and should be defrosted in the refrigerator for at least 3 hours or overnight first.

When ready to bake the cookies, position a rack in the middle of the oven. Preheat the oven to 350°F/180°C/gas 4. Line two baking sheets with parchment paper.

Use a large, sharp knife to cut each cold log into 12 slices about ½ in/12 mm thick. Place the cookies 2 in/5 cm apart on the baking sheets. Sprinkle a few grains of sea salt (about 10 to 12) over each cookie.

Bake the cookies one sheet at a time just until the tops begin to crackle slightly and feel firm if touched lightly, about 20 minutes.

Let cool on the baking sheet for 10 minutes. Use a wide metal spatula to transfer the cookies to a wire rack to cool completely.

The cookies can be stored in a tightly covered container at room temperature for up to 3 days.

CHOCOLATE-DIPPED PEANUT BUTTER *cookies*

An entire cup of peanut butter is a lot more than the usual peanut butter cookie recipe includes, but these cookies set a new standard. I say if you're making peanut butter cookies, the taste of peanut butter should prevail, and prevail it does in these crisp cookies.

MEASURING & MIXING TIME *15 minutes*

BAKE AT *350°F/180°C/gas 4* FOR ABOUT *13 minutes*

COOKIES

1 ½ cups/185 g unbleached all-purpose flour

½ tsp baking soda

¼ tsp salt

½ cup/115 g unsalted butter, at room temperature

½ cup/100 g firmly packed dark brown sugar

½ cup/100 g granulated sugar

1 cup/250 g smooth peanut butter, at room temperature

1 egg

1 tsp vanilla extract

MILK CHOCOLATE COATING

12 oz/340 g milk chocolate, chopped

2 tbsp canola or corn oil

Make the cookies. Sift the flour, baking soda, and salt into a medium bowl. Set aside.

Put the butter, brown sugar, and granulated sugar in the bowl of an electric mixer and beat on medium speed until smoothly blended, about 1 minute. Stop the mixer and scrape the sides of the bowl as needed. Mix in the peanut butter until blended, about 1 minute. Mix in the egg and vanilla until blended, about 1 minute. Reduce the speed to low, add the flour mixture, and mix just until incorporated.

Divide the dough into two equal parts. Put each on a large piece of plastic wrap and form into a log 7 in/17 cm long and 1½ in/4 cm in diameter. Roll each back and forth to form a smooth cylinder, then wrap in the plastic wrap. Refrigerate for at least 3 hours or overnight, until firm, or wrap aluminum foil over the plastic wrap and freeze for up to 2 months.

Frozen dough will be difficult to cut and should be defrosted in the refrigerator for at least 3 hours or overnight first.

When ready to bake the cookies, position a rack in the middle of the oven. Preheat the oven to 350°F/180°C/gas 4. Line two baking sheets with parchment paper.

Use a large, sharp knife to cut each cold log into 14 slices about ½ in/12 mm thick. Place the cookies 2½ in/6 cm apart on the baking sheets. Use the tines of a fork to press a cross-hatch pattern on top of each cookie.

Bake the cookies one sheet at a time just until the tops feel firm if touched lightly, about 13 minutes.

Let cool on the baking sheet for 10 minutes. Use a wide metal spatula to transfer the cookies to a wire rack to cool completely. The cookies become crisp as they cool.

Make the coating. Put the chocolate and oil in a heatproof bowl or the top of a double boiler and place it over a saucepan of barely simmering water or the bottom of the double boiler; the water should not touch the bowl. Stir until the chocolate is melted and smooth. Scrape the mixture into a medium bowl and set aside for about 5 minutes to cool and thicken slightly.

Spread out a large piece of wax paper. Sweep the top of each cookie through the chocolate coating, covering about half of the top surface. Place the cookies on the wax paper and let sit until the chocolate coating is firm, about 1 hour at room temperature, or sooner if refrigerated. You will have some chocolate coating left over for another use, but the larger quantity makes it easier to coat the cookies.

The cookies can be stored between layers of wax paper in a tightly covered container at room temperature for up to 3 days. If the kitchen temperature is warm, store them in the refrigerator to keep the chocolate firm.

CHOICES

- *Roll the shaped logs in chopped peanuts before wrapping and refrigerating.*
- *Sprinkle chopped unsalted peanuts over the sliced cookies just before baking.*
- *Leave the baked cookies plain, with no chocolate coating.*

CHOCOLATE & PEPPERMINT-CRUNCH *cookies*

Look no further for a festive cookie to adorn the holiday cookie platter. These dark chocolate cookies are topped with crushed peppermint candy that's attached to the cookies with drizzles of chocolate coating. I leave the peppermint candy in its wrapper and crush it with the flat side of a meat pounder or hammer. Remove the plastic covering after crushing it. The yield of this recipe is somewhat smaller than for most of the recipes in this book, making only one 10-in/25-cm log. However, the ingredients can easily be doubled to make two logs and forty cookies.

MEASURING & MIXING TIME *20 minutes*

BAKE AT *350°F/180°C/gas 4* FOR ABOUT *15 minutes*

COOKIES

1 cup/125 g unbleached all-purpose flour

¼ cup/20 g unsweetened Dutch-process cocoa powder

½ tsp baking soda

¼ tsp salt

½ cup/115 g unsalted butter, melted

¼ cup/50 g firmly packed light brown sugar

6 tbsp/75 g granulated sugar

1 tbsp water

1 tsp vanilla extract

⅔ cup/115 g semisweet miniature chocolate chips

CHOCOLATE COATING

4 oz/115 g semisweet chocolate, chopped

1 tbsp canola or corn oil

---

3 oz/85 g peppermint candy canes or peppermint hard candy, coarsely crushed

Make the cookies. Sift the flour, cocoa powder, baking soda, and salt into a medium bowl. Set aside.

Put the melted butter, brown sugar, granulated sugar, water, and vanilla in the bowl of an electric mixer and mix on low speed until smoothly blended, about 1 minute. Stop the mixer and scrape the sides of the bowl as needed. Add the flour mixture and mix just until incorporated. Add the chocolate chips and mix just until evenly distributed.

Put the dough on a large piece of plastic wrap and form into a log 10 in/25 cm long and 1½ in/4 cm in diameter. Roll it back and forth to form a smooth cylinder, then wrap in the plastic wrap. Refrigerate for at least 3 hours or overnight, until firm, or wrap aluminum foil over the plastic wrap and freeze for up to 2 months.

Frozen dough will be difficult to cut and should be defrosted in the refrigerator for at least 3 hours or overnight first.

When ready to bake the cookies, position a rack in the middle of the oven. Preheat the oven to 350°F/180°C/gas 4. Line two baking sheets with parchment paper.

Use a large, sharp knife to cut the cold log into 20 slices about ½ in/12 mm thick. Place the cookies 3 in/7.5 cm apart on the baking sheets.

Bake the cookies one sheet at a time just until the tops are beginning to crack and feel firm if touched lightly, about 15 minutes.

Let cool on the baking sheet for 10 minutes. Use a wide metal spatula to transfer the cookies to a wire rack to cool completely.

Make the coating. Put the chocolate and oil in a heatproof bowl or the top of a double boiler and place it over a saucepan of barely simmering water or the bottom of the double boiler; the water should not touch the bowl. Stir until the chocolate is melted and smooth. Scrape the mixture into a medium bowl and set aside for about 5 minutes to cool and thicken slightly.

Sprinkle some of the crushed peppermint candy over the top of each cookie. Use a small spoon to drizzle the chocolate coating over the cookies, coating the candy with thin drizzles of chocolate. Let sit until the chocolate coating is firm, about 1 hour at room temperature, or sooner if refrigerated.

The cookies can be stored between layers of wax paper in a tightly covered container at room temperature for up to 3 days. If the kitchen temperature is warm, store them in the refrigerator to keep the chocolate firm.

CHOICES

- *For cookies that are slightly soft in the center, bake for just 12 minutes; the tops should still feel soft in the center if lightly touched.*
- *Substitute crushed toffee candy for the peppermint candy.*
- *Forgo the peppermint candy and simply drizzle the cookies with chocolate coating.*
- *In addition to the dark chocolate coating, make a white chocolate coating using the same quantities (4 oz/115 g of white chocolate and 1 tbsp oil). Drizzle both coatings over each cookie.*

NEAPOLITAN STRIPED *crisps*

Remember those half gallons of Neapolitan ice cream? They contained stripes of chocolate, strawberry, and vanilla flavors. In these cookies, a plain, vanilla dough is divided into three parts, then one part is flavored with chocolate and another part with strawberry. The three flavors are then layered in a small loaf pan to create a striped cookie that imitates the ice cream. They are a great choice to serve with any flavor of ice cream. Try placing a cookie sticking up from a scoop of ice cream.

   I recommend using aluminum foil mini loaf pans, especially if you plan to freeze any of the dough for an extended period of time. I use strawberry fruit spread in these cookies. It has no added sugar and is smooth. Strawberry jam will work, but it should be processed in a food processor or blender to make it smooth.

MEASURING & MIXING TIME *10 minutes*

BAKE AT *350°F/180°C/gas 4* FOR ABOUT *14 minutes*

2 oz/55 g semisweet chocolate, chopped

2 cups/255 g unbleached all-purpose flour

½ tsp baking powder

¼ tsp salt

1 cup/225 g unsalted butter, at room temperature

1 cup/200 g sugar

2 egg yolks

1 tsp vanilla extract

1 tbsp unsweetened Dutch-process cocoa powder, sifted

5 tbsp plus 2 tsp/120 g strawberry fruit spread

Line two aluminum foil mini loaf pans measuring about 5 in/12 cm long by 3 in/7.5 cm wide with plastic wrap, letting the wrap extend over the ends of the pan.

Put the chocolate in a heatproof bowl or the top of a double boiler and place it over a saucepan of barely simmering water or the bottom of the double boiler; the water should not touch the bowl. Stir until the chocolate is melted and smooth. Set aside to cool slightly.

Sift the flour, baking powder, and salt into a medium bowl. Set aside.

Put the butter and sugar in the bowl of an electric mixer and beat on medium speed until smoothly blended, about 1 minute. Stop the mixer and scrape the sides of the bowl as needed. Mix in the egg yolks and vanilla until blended, about 1 minute. Reduce the speed to low, add the flour mixture, and mix just until incorporated.

Divide the dough into three equal portions, each about 1 cup/225 g, leaving one portion in the mixing bowl. Transfer the two remaining portions to two clean bowls. Add the melted chocolate and cocoa powder to the dough in the mixer bowl and mix on low speed to form a smooth chocolate dough. Use a large spoon to stir 3 tbsp of the strawberry spread into one bowl of dough until smoothly blended. Leave the remaining portion as is for vanilla dough. *continued…*

Divide each flavor of dough into two equal parts. Press one piece of chocolate dough into the bottom of a prepared pan, using the back of a spoon to smooth the top. Spread 2 tsp of the strawberry spread over the dough. Spread one piece of the strawberry dough on top and spread 2 tsp of the strawberry spread over it. Spread one piece of vanilla dough on top. Repeat with the remaining three pieces of dough and strawberry spread, layering them in the second prepared pan in the same way. Wrap the overhanging edges of plastic wrap over the top, then wrap each pan in plastic wrap. Refrigerate for at least 5 hours or overnight, until firm, or wrap aluminum foil over the plastic wrap and freeze in the pans for up to 2 months.

Frozen dough will be difficult to cut and should be defrosted in the refrigerator for at least 3 hours or overnight first.

When ready to bake the cookies, position a rack in the middle of the oven. Preheat the oven to 350°F/180°C/gas 4. Line two baking sheets with parchment paper.

Remove the cold stack of dough from the loaf pan by lifting the plastic wrap. Use a large, sharp knife to cut each stack into 20 slices about ¼ in/6 mm thick. These are tall slices, and it's important to cut straight down through the dough to make slices of even thickness. Place the cookies 1½ in/4 cm apart on the baking sheets.

Bake the cookies one sheet at a time until the edges begin to brown, about 14 minutes.

Let cool on the baking sheet for 10 minutes. Use a wide metal spatula to transfer the cookies to a wire rack to cool completely.

The cookies can be stored in a tightly covered container at room temperature for up to 4 days.

CHOICES

- *Seedless raspberry jam can be substituted for the strawberry fruit spread.*
- *To make sandwich cookies from these large cookies, cut them in half before baking. After baking, sandwich them together with strawberry fruit spread or Chocolate Ganache (pages 82 and 84).*

DOUBLE-SPIRAL CINNAMON *crisps*

The many buttery layers of these cookies are produced by a quick sour cream dough that mimics puff pastry. The dough is rolled up with cinnamon sugar to make fancy cookies that look as if they took hours to prepare, rather than minutes. But who's telling? Not me.

MEASURING & MIXING TIME *15 minutes*

BAKE AT *350°F/180°C/gas 4* FOR ABOUT *17 minutes*

¼ cup sugar

1 ¼ tsp ground cinnamon

1 cup/125 g unbleached all-purpose flour

½ cup plus 2 tbsp/145 g cold unsalted butter, cut into pieces

⅓ cup/80 ml cold sour cream

1 tsp vanilla extract

In a small bowl, stir the sugar and cinnamon together until evenly blended. Set aside.

Put the flour and butter in the bowl of an electric mixer and mix on low speed until the butter is in pieces the size of small lima beans, about 45 seconds. The butter pieces will be different sizes, and there will be some loose flour. With the mixer running, add the sour cream and vanilla and mix just until the dough holds together in large, smooth clumps that pull away from the sides of the bowl, about 30 seconds. The dough will be cold and can be rolled right away. Gather the dough together and pat it into a flat rectangular shape.

Transfer the dough to a lightly floured work surface and, using a floured rolling pin, roll it out to a rectangle 18 in/ 46 cm long and 16 in/40.5 cm wide, with a short side facing you. This is a large piece, but it's easier to roll up as one piece. Leaving a 1-in/2.5-cm bare edge along both long edges and reserving 1 tbsp of the cinnamon sugar, sprinkle the remaining cinnamon sugar evenly over the dough.

Beginning at the bottom edge, roll the dough up tightly, but stop when you reach the halfway point. Then, beginning at the top, roll the dough tightly toward the center until the second roll meets the first one. Pinch the seam along the length of the roll to seal it tightly. Pinch the ends to seal them tightly. Sprinkle the reserved cinnamon sugar evenly over the roll and roll it back and forth to coat the outside with cinnamon sugar. The finished roll should shrink to about 12 in/30.5 cm in length.

Cut the roll in half crosswise to form two pieces, each 6 in/ 15 cm long. Wrap each piece in a large piece of plastic wrap. Refrigerate for at least 3 hours or overnight, until firm, or wrap aluminum foil over the plastic wrap and freeze for up to 2 months.

Frozen dough will be difficult to cut and should be defrosted in the refrigerator for at least 3 hours or overnight first. ***continued…***

DOUBLE-SPIRAL CINNAMON *crisps (continued)*

When ready to bake the cookies, position a rack in the middle of the oven. Preheat the oven to 350°F/180°C/gas 4. Line two baking sheets with parchment paper.

Use a large, sharp knife to cut each cold log into 18 slices about ⅓ in/8 mm thick. Place the cookies 1½ in/4 cm apart on the baking sheets.

Bake the cookies one sheet at a time just until light brown, about 17 minutes. The cookies will spread into large, open double spirals as they bake.

Let cool on the baking sheet for 10 minutes. Use a wide metal spatula to transfer the cookies to a wire rack to cool completely.

The cookies can be stored in a tightly covered container at room temperature for up to 3 days.

CHOICES

Substitute plain sugar for the cinnamon sugar.

DATE & PECAN *pinwheels*

MAKES **60**

My friend Carol Witham shared her favorite slice and bake recipe with me. During mixing the brown sugar dough has an appealing scent that signals the good cookies to come. The dough is rolled up with a date and pecan filling that forms an attractive pinwheel pattern when sliced into cookies. Be sure to the cool the filling before spreading it on the dough. If hot, the filling will soften the dough and make it sticky and difficult to roll up. To cut up the dates easily and prevent sticking, use an oiled knife or oiled, clean scissors.

MEASURING & MIXING TIME *20 minutes*

BAKE AT *350°F/180°C/gas 4* FOR ABOUT *12 minutes*

FILLING

1 ⅓ cups/225 g pitted dates, cut into ⅓-in/8-mm pieces

¼ cup/60 ml water

¼ cup/50 g sugar

½ cup/55 g pecans, finely chopped

COOKIES

2 cups/255 g unbleached all-purpose flour

½ tsp baking soda

¼ tsp salt

½ cup/115 g unsalted butter, at room temperature

1 cup/200 g firmly packed light brown sugar

1 egg

1 egg yolk

1 tsp vanilla extract

Make the filling. Put the dates, water, and sugar in a small saucepan over medium heat and bring to a simmer. Decrease the heat to medium-low, cover, and simmer for 10 minutes. Remove from the heat, stir in the pecans, and leave uncovered to cool to room temperature. Cover after 30 minutes.

Make the cookies. Sift the flour, baking soda, and salt into a medium bowl. Set aside.

Put the butter and brown sugar in the bowl of an electric mixer and beat on medium speed until smoothly blended, about 1 minute. Stop the mixer and scrape the sides of the bowl as needed. Mix in the egg, egg yolk, and vanilla until blended, about 1 minute. Reduce the speed to low, add the flour mixture, and mix just until incorporated.

Divide the dough into two equal parts. Put each on a large piece of plastic wrap and form into a square slab 5 in/12 cm across. Wrap in the plastic wrap. Refrigerate for at least 3 hours or overnight.

Remove one piece of dough from the refrigerator, unwrap it, and put it between two large pieces of wax paper. Roll the dough out to a rectangle 10 in/25 cm long and 8 in/20 cm wide. Remove the top piece of wax paper. Leaving a bare edge ¾ in/2 cm wide all the way around, drop half of the filling over the surface in small dollops, then use your fingers to gently spread the filling in a thin, even layer over the dough, still keeping the edges bare. Starting from a long side, use the bottom piece of wax paper to help roll the dough up into a tight log, removing the wax paper as you go. Wrap the cylinder in plastic wrap. Repeat with the second piece of dough and the remaining filling. Refrigerate for at least 3 hours or overnight, until firm, or wrap aluminum foil over the plastic wrap and freeze for up to 2 months.

Frozen dough will be difficult to cut and should be defrosted in the refrigerator for at least 3 hours or overnight first.

When ready to bake the cookies, position a rack in the middle of the oven. Preheat the oven to 350°F/180°C/gas 4. Line two or three baking sheets with parchment paper.

Use a large, sharp knife to cut each cold log into 30 slices about ⅓ in/8 mm thick. Place the cookies 1 in/2.5 cm apart on the baking sheets. (These cookies don't spread much.)

Bake the cookies one sheet at a time just until they begin to brown and the tops feel firm if touched lightly, about 12 minutes.

Let cool on the baking sheet for 10 minutes. Use a wide metal spatula to transfer the cookies to a wire rack to cool completely.

The cookies can be stored in a tightly covered container at room temperature for up to 3 days.

STUFFED & SANDWICH COOKIES

You might think of the cookies in this chapter as "super cookies." Two cookies with a filling sealed inside or sandwiched together with filling squishing out of the edges—who wouldn't want that? Anyone I know would. Whether filled before or after baking, two cookies are better than one.

Stuffed cookies, which are filled before being baked, have a filling sealed between two cookie dough slices. Press the edges of dough together with your fingers or a fork to seal them and enjoy the surprise inside after they bake. Chocolate (of course), peanut butter, dried fruits, or chopped nuts are some of the possibilities for fillings.

Sandwich cookies have the filling added after the cookies are baked, which allows them to hold more filling than stuffed cookies can. Chocolate, thick chocolate sauce, caramel, and frosting are some possibilities for filling sandwich cookies. Some of these sandwich cookies have shapes cut out of the dough slices before baking. Use small cookies cutters such as gingerbread people, hearts, stars, trees, letters, or whatever shape strikes your fancy. For these cookies, half of the cookies remain uncut and serve as the base; the cookies with the cutouts are placed on top, allowing the filling to show through. The small cutouts, which are baked separately, make fun snacks.

RAISIN-FILLED CINNAMON *cookies*

MAKES 20

Cinnamon must be one of the best-liked spices, and cinnamon and raisins one of the most popular combinations. That was my inspiration for this recipe, where cinnamon cookies are stuffed with a cinnamon and raisin filling. A cinnamon sugar topping is the perfect finishing touch.

MEASURING & MIXING TIME *10 minutes*

BAKE AT *350°F/180°C/gas 4* FOR ABOUT *16 minutes*

COOKIES

2 cups/255 g unbleached all-purpose flour

½ tsp baking powder

½ tsp baking soda

¼ tsp salt

1 tsp ground cinnamon

1 cup/225 g unsalted butter, at room temperature

1 cup/200 g sugar

1 egg

1 egg yolk

1 tsp vanilla extract

FILLING

½ cup/85 g seedless raisins, finely chopped

1 tbsp plus 1 tsp firmly packed light brown sugar

½ tsp ground cinnamon

¼ tsp ground nutmeg

3 tbsp sour cream

TOPPING (OPTIONAL)

2 tbsp sugar

½ tsp ground cinnamon

Make the cookies. Sift the flour, baking powder, baking soda, salt, and cinnamon into a medium bowl. Set aside.

Put the butter and sugar in the bowl of an electric mixer and beat on medium speed until smoothly blended, about 1 minute. Stop the mixer and scrape the sides of the bowl as needed. Mix in the egg, egg yolk, and vanilla until blended, about 1 minute. Reduce the speed to low, add the flour mixture, and mix just until incorporated.

Divide the dough into two equal parts. Put each on a large piece of plastic wrap and form into a log 5 in/12 cm long and 1¾ in/4.5 cm in diameter. Roll each back and forth to form a smooth cylinder, then wrap in the plastic wrap. Refrigerate for at least 3 hours or overnight, until firm, or wrap aluminum foil over the plastic wrap and freeze for up to 2 months.

Frozen dough will be difficult to cut and should be defrosted in the refrigerator for at least 3 hours or overnight first.

When ready to bake the cookies, position a rack in the middle of the oven. Preheat the oven to 350°F/180°C/gas 4. Line two baking sheets with parchment paper.

Make the filling. In a small bowl, stir the raisins, brown sugar, cinnamon, nutmeg, and sour cream together until well combined.

Use a large, sharp knife to cut each cold log into 20 slices about ¼ in/6 mm thick. Place half of the cookies 2 in/5 cm apart on the baking sheets. Put 1 tsp of filling in the center of each. Top each with another cookie. Use the tines of a fork to press the edges together to seal them. The cookies may crack slightly on top. This is fine; the filling won't leak.

Make the topping, if desired. In a small bowl, stir the sugar and cinnamon together until evenly blended.

Use a pastry brush to lightly coat the top of each cookie with water, then sprinkle the cinnamon sugar evenly over the cookies.

Bake the cookies one sheet at a time just until the tops are lightly browned and feel firm if touched lightly, about 16 minutes.

Let cool on the baking sheet for 10 minutes. Use a wide metal spatula to transfer the cookies to a wire rack to cool completely.

The cookies can be stored in a tightly covered container at room temperature for up to 3 days.

CHOICES

• *Substitute other finely chopped dried fruits, such as apricots, dates, or figs, for the raisins.*
• *Substitute finely chopped nuts for some of the dried fruit in the filling.*

PEANUT BUTTER *cookies stuffed with chocolate & peanut butter*

MAKES 24

There is a nice surprise inside these soft and buttery peanut butter rounds (see photo, page 66). The cookies enclose a delicious filling of milk chocolate and peanut butter, which melt together during baking to create a flavor reminiscent of a peanut butter cup.

MEASURING & MIXING TIME *15 minutes*

BAKE AT *350°F/180°C/gas 4* FOR ABOUT *12 minutes*

COOKIES

1 ½ cups/185 g unbleached all-purpose flour

1 tsp baking soda

¼ tsp salt

½ cup/115 g unsalted butter, at room temperature

¾ cup/150 g firmly packed dark brown sugar

¼ cup/50 g granulated sugar

¼ cup/65 g smooth peanut butter, at room temperature

1 egg

1 tsp vanilla extract

FILLING

2 tbsp smooth peanut butter

2 tsp powdered sugar

Two 1.55-oz/44-g milk chocolate candy bars (such as Hershey's Milk Chocolate bars)

Powdered sugar for dusting (optional)

Make the cookies. Sift the flour, baking soda, and salt into a medium bowl. Set aside.

Put the butter, brown sugar, and granulated sugar in the bowl of an electric mixer and beat on medium speed until smoothly blended, about 1 minute. Stop the mixer and scrape the sides of the bowl as needed. Mix in the peanut butter until blended, about 30 seconds. Mix in the egg and vanilla until blended, about 1 minute. Reduce the speed to low, add the flour mixture, and mix just until incorporated.

Divide the dough into two equal parts. Put each on a large piece of plastic wrap and form into a roughly shaped log 6 in/15 cm long and 1½ in/4 cm in diameter. Roll each back and forth to form a smooth cylinder, then wrap in the plastic wrap. Refrigerate for about 30 minutes, then roll each log again to form a more uniformly shaped cylinder. Refrigerate for at least 2½ hours or overnight, until firm, or wrap aluminum foil over the plastic wrap and freeze for up to 2 months.

Frozen dough will be difficult to cut and should be defrosted in the refrigerator for at least 3 hours or overnight first.

When ready to bake the cookies, position a rack in the middle of the oven. Preheat the oven to 350°F/180°C/gas 4. Line two baking sheets with parchment paper.

Make the filling. In a small bowl, stir the peanut butter and powdered sugar together until evenly blended. Spread half of the mixture evenly over each candy bar. Cut each candy bar into 12 equal pieces to make a total of 24 peanut butter–covered pieces of chocolate.

Use a large, sharp knife to cut each cold log of dough into 24 slices about ¼ in/6 mm thick. Place half of the cookies 2 in/5 cm apart on the baking sheets. Place one piece of the peanut butter-covered chocolate bar pieces in the center of each. Top each with another cookie. Use your fingers to press the edges together to seal them.

Bake the cookies one sheet at a time just until they darken slightly and the tops feel firm if touched lightly, about 12 minutes.

Let cool on the baking sheets for 10 minutes. Use a wide metal spatula to transfer the cookies to a wire rack to cool completely. Dust with powdered sugar, if desired.

The cookies can be stored in a tightly covered container at room temperature for up to 3 days.

CHOCOLATE-ALMOND *bull's-eyes*

MAKES **84**

These cookies, which are both chewy and crisp, have soft, cream-colored almond cookie dough in the center, surrounded by a dark chocolate cookie border. These cookies require a bit of additional advance planning, as the doughlike almond filling is frozen before the chocolate dough is wrapped around it. This makes it easy to press the soft chocolate dough neatly onto and around the almond filling.

MEASURING & MIXING TIME *10 minutes*

BAKE AT *325°F/165°C/gas 3* FOR ABOUT *17 minutes*

ALMOND DOUGH

8 oz/225 g almond paste

2 tbsp unsalted butter, at room temperature

⅓ cup/65 g sugar

¼ cup/30 g unbleached all-purpose flour

1 egg white

1 tbsp fresh lemon juice

½ tsp vanilla extract

CHOCOLATE DOUGH

2 cups/255 g unbleached all-purpose flour

6 tbsp/35 g unsweetened Dutch-process cocoa powder

½ tsp salt

1 cup/225 g unsalted butter, at room temperature

1 cup/100 g powdered sugar

1 tsp vanilla extract

Make the almond dough. In a food processor, process the almond paste and butter until smooth. Add the sugar, flour, egg white, lemon juice, and vanilla and process until smooth. Divide the mixture into three equal parts. Put each on a large piece of plastic wrap and form into a log about 7 in/17 cm long and ¾ in/2 cm in diameter. Roll each log up in plastic wrap. Freeze for at least 5 hours or overnight, until firm.

Make the chocolate dough. Sift the flour, cocoa powder, and salt into a medium bowl and set aside.

Put the butter, powdered sugar, and vanilla in the bowl of an electric mixer and beat on medium speed until smoothly blended, about 1 minute. Reduce the speed to low, add the flour mixture, and mix just until incorporated.

Divide the dough into six equal parts and roll them into logs about 7 in/17 cm long. The dough will be soft. Two of the chocolate logs will be pressed around each almond log to surround it.

Remove one almond log from the freezer and unwrap it. Place the almond log on top of one chocolate log and place another chocolate log on top of the almond log. Press on the top piece of dough to flatten the soft chocolate dough slightly, then press the chocolate dough around the almond log to evenly cover it with chocolate dough. Wrap in plastic wrap and roll back and forth to form a smooth cylinder.

Repeat with the remaining dough. Refrigerate for at least 2 hours or overnight, until firm, or wrap aluminum foil around the plastic wrap and freeze for up to 2 months.

Frozen dough will be difficult to cut and should be defrosted in the refrigerator for at least 3 hours or overnight first.

When ready to bake the cookies, position a rack in the middle of the oven. Preheat the oven to 325°F/165°C/gas 3. Line two or three baking sheets with parchment paper.

Remove one log of dough from the refrigerator. Use a large, sharp knife to cut it into 28 slices about ¼ in/6 mm thick. Place the cookies 1 in/2.5 cm apart on the baking sheets. (These cookies don't spread much.) Repeat with the remaining logs of dough.

Bake the cookies one sheet at a time until the centers color slightly and the edges feel firm if touched lightly, about 17 minutes.

Let cool on the baking sheet for 10 minutes. Use a wide spatula to carefully transfer the cookies to a wire rack to cool completely. The centers will remain soft and slightly chewy, but the chocolate edges will become crisp as the cookies cool.

The cookies can be stored in a tightly covered container at room temperature for up to 3 days.

LEMON SANDWICH *cookies*

MAKES **24**

Recently I brought a platter of assorted cookies to a lunch party. Several people spotted these sandwich cookies and asked if they were lemon. When I said they were, that was the last I saw of those cookies.

MEASURING & MIXING TIME *10 minutes*

BAKE AT *350°F/180°C/gas 4* FOR ABOUT *15 minutes*

COOKIES
1 cup/225 g unsalted butter, at room temperature

⅓ cup/65 g sugar

¼ tsp salt

1 egg yolk

1 tsp grated lemon zest

1 tbsp fresh lemon juice

1 tsp vanilla extract

¼ tsp almond extract

1 cup plus 2 tbsp/140 g unbleached all-purpose flour

FILLING
6 tbsp/85 g unsalted butter, at room temperature

1 cup/100 g powdered sugar

1 tsp grated lemon zest

2 tsp fresh lemon juice

1 tsp vanilla extract

Make the cookies. Put the butter, sugar, and salt in the bowl of an electric mixer and beat on medium speed until smoothly blended, about 1 minute. Stop the mixer and scrape the sides of the bowl as needed. Mix in the egg yolk, lemon zest, lemon juice, vanilla, and almond extract until blended, about 1 minute. Reduce the speed to low, add the flour, and mix just until a smooth dough forms and starts to come away from the sides of the bowl, about 1 minute.

Divide the dough into two equal parts. Put each on a large piece of plastic wrap and form into a log 6 in/15 cm long and 1¼ in/3 cm in diameter. Roll each back and forth to form a smooth cylinder, then wrap in the plastic wrap. Refrigerate for at least 3 hours or overnight, until firm, or wrap aluminum foil over the plastic wrap and freeze for up to 2 months.

Frozen dough will be difficult to cut and should be defrosted in the refrigerator for at least 3 hours or overnight first.

When ready to bake the cookies, position a rack in the middle of the oven. Preheat the oven to 350°F/180°C/gas 4. Line two baking sheets with parchment paper.

Use a large, sharp knife to cut each cold log into 24 slices about ¼ in/6 mm thick. Place the cookies 1 in/2.5 cm apart on the baking sheets. (These cookies don't spread much.)

Bake the cookies one sheet at a time just until the edges begin to brown but the centers remain pale, about 15 minutes.

Let cool on the baking sheet for 10 minutes. Use a wide metal spatula to transfer the cookies to a wire rack to cool.

Make the filling. In a medium bowl, stir the butter, powdered sugar, and lemon zest together until crumbly. Add the lemon juice and vanilla and stir until smooth and creamy.

Turn half of the cookies flat-side up and spread about 1 tsp of filling in the center of each. Top with the remaining cookies, flat-side down, and gently press to spread the filling.

The cookies can be stored between layers of wax paper in a tightly covered container in the refrigerator for up to 3 days.

ORANGE-SCENTED *alfajores*

When my friend Adia Wright found out about this book, she immediately offered to share her recipe for *alfajores*, an Argentinean specialty in which two butter cookies are sandwiched together with dulce de leche. The final touch is rolling the edges of the cookies in unsweetened shredded coconut. Adia's secret is including some Grand Marnier in the cookie dough to add a subtle orange liqueur flavor. When Adia's Argentine grandmother-in-law tasted her cookies, she said they were better than the ones she had been baking for years. High praise indeed!

Dulce de leche is a caramel sauce made by cooking sweetened condensed milk over low heat for a long time, until it caramelizes. It is available at South American markets and from Williams-Sonoma and Stonewall Kitchen (www.w-s.com and www.stonewallkitchen.com). A large ratio of cornstarch is used in these cookies; because it has no gluten, this makes the cookies especially tender.

MEASURING & MIXING TIME *15 minutes*

BAKE AT *325°F/165°C/gas 3* **FOR ABOUT** *23 minutes*

1 ½ cups/170 g cornstarch

1 ½ cups/185 g unbleached all-purpose flour

½ tsp baking powder

¼ tsp salt

1 cup/225 g unsalted butter, at room temperature

1 cup/200 g sugar

1 egg

2 egg yolks

2 tbsp Grand Marnier or other orange liqueur

1 ½ tsp vanilla extract

1 tsp grated lemon zest

¾ cup plus 2 tbsp/210 ml dulce de leche

1 ½ cups/150 g unsweetened dried shredded coconut

Sift the cornstarch, flour, baking powder, and salt into a medium bowl. Set aside.

Put the butter and sugar in the bowl of an electric mixer and beat on medium speed until smoothly blended, about 1 minute. Stop the mixer and scrape the sides of the bowl as needed. Mix in the egg, egg yolks, Grand Marnier, vanilla, and lemon zest until blended, about 1 minute. Reduce the speed to low, add the flour mixture, and mix just until incorporated.

Divide the dough into two equal parts. Put each on a large piece of plastic wrap and form into a log 5 in/12 cm long and 2 in/5 cm in diameter. Roll each back and forth to form a smooth cylinder, then wrap in the plastic wrap. Refrigerate for at least 3 hours or overnight, until firm, or wrap aluminum foil over the plastic wrap and freeze for up to 2 months.

Frozen dough will be difficult to cut and should be defrosted in the refrigerator for at least 3 hours or overnight first. *continued…*

ORANGE-SCENTED *alfajores (continued)*

When ready to bake the cookies, position a rack in the middle of the oven. Preheat the oven to 325°F/165°C/gas 3. Line two baking sheets with parchment paper.

Use a large, sharp knife to cut each cold log into 20 slices about ¼ in/6 mm thick. Place the cookies 2 in/5 cm apart on the baking sheets.

Bake the cookies one sheet at a time just until the tops feel firm if touched lightly, about 23 minutes.

Let cool on the baking sheet for 10 minutes. Use a wide metal spatula to transfer the cookies to a wire rack to cool completely.

Turn half of the cookies flat-side up and spread about 2 tsp dulce de leche over each. Top with the remaining cookies, flat-side down, and gently press to spread the filling, allowing some of the dulce de leche to squeeze out the sides.

Pour the coconut onto a large piece of wax paper. Dip the edges of each cookie in the coconut to coat the edges all the way around. You will have some coconut left over for another use, but the larger quantity makes it easier to coat the cookies.

The cookies can be stored between layers of wax paper in a tightly covered container at room temperature for up to 3 days. If the kitchen temperature is warm, store them in the refrigerator to prevent the dulce de leche from oozing out.

HAZELNUT SHORTBREAD SQUARES
with Nutella filling

MAKES 30

I used to return from vacations in Italy with jars of Nutella. Nowadays the chocolate hazelnut spread is in American supermarkets, and it's an excellent filling for these cookies.

MEASURING & MIXING TIME *15 minutes*

BAKE AT *375°F/190°C/gas 5* FOR ABOUT *13 minutes*

1 ¾ cups/215 g unbleached all-purpose flour

½ tsp baking powder

¼ tsp salt

½ cup/55 g cornstarch

½ cup/55 g hazelnuts, skinned and toasted (see page 12)

1 cup/225 g unsalted butter, at room temperature

⅔ cup/130 g granulated sugar

2 tsp vanilla extract

3 tbsp skinned, toasted, and chopped hazelnuts (see page 12)

1 cup/300 g Nutella, at room temperature

Sift the flour, baking powder, and salt into a medium bowl. Set aside.

In a food processor, pulse the cornstarch and hazelnuts to combine, then process until the hazelnuts are finely ground. A mini food processor works well.

Put the butter, granulated sugar, and vanilla in the bowl of an electric mixer and beat on medium speed until blended, about 1 minute. Stop the mixer and scrape the sides of the bowl as needed. Reduce the speed to low, add the hazelnut mixture, and mix until evenly blended. Add the flour mixture, and mix just until a rough dough forms and starts to come away from the sides of the bowl, about 1 minute.

Divide the dough into two equal parts. Put each on a large piece of plastic wrap and form into a square log 7½ in/19 cm long and 1½ in/4 cm square at the ends. Wrap in the plastic wrap and rotate the wrapped dough, patting it on all four sides to form long, straight, even edges. Refrigerate for at least 3 hours or overnight, until firm, or wrap aluminum foil over the plastic wrap and freeze for up to 2 months.

Frozen dough will be difficult to cut and should be defrosted in the refrigerator for at least 3 hours or overnight first.

When ready to bake the cookies, position a rack in the middle of the oven. Preheat the oven to 375°F/190°C/gas 5. Line two baking sheets with parchment paper.

Use a large, sharp knife to cut each cold log into 30 slices about ¼ in/6 mm thick. Place the cookies 1 in/2.5 cm apart on the baking sheets. (These cookies don't spread much.) Lightly sprinkle the cookies with the chopped hazelnuts, gently pressing them into the dough.

Bake the cookies one sheet at a time just until the edges and bottoms are lightly browned, about 13 minutes.

Let cool on the baking sheet for 10 minutes. Use a wide metal spatula to transfer the cookies to a wire rack to cool completely.

Turn half of the cookies flat-side up and spread about 1½ tsp of Nutella in the center of each. Top with the remaining cookies, flat-side down, and gently press to spread the filling.

The cookies can be stored between layers of wax paper in a tightly covered container at room temperature for up to 3 days.

SANDWICH COOKIES *with caramel filling & crunchy pecans*

Brown sugar cookies, salty maple pecan crunch, and sticky caramel filling—that should provide sufficient temptation to make these cookies. The pecans are mixed with maple syrup and salt and transform into a crunchy topping as the cookies bake. Making the caramel sauce is easy; just be careful not to burn the sugar or yourself.

MEASURING & MIXING TIME *20 minutes*

BAKE AT *325°F/165°C/gas 3* FOR ABOUT *17 minutes*

COOKIES
¾ cup/90 g unbleached all-purpose flour

¼ cup/30 g cake flour

½ tsp salt

¾ tsp ground cinnamon

½ cup plus 2 tbsp/145 g unsalted butter, at room temperature

½ cup/100 g firmly packed light brown sugar

1 tsp vanilla extract

TOPPING
½ cup/55 g pecans, coarsely chopped

1 ½ tsp maple syrup

¼ tsp salt

FILLING
⅔ cup/160 ml heavy cream

1 cup/200 g sugar

½ cup/120 ml water

Make the cookies. Sift the all-purpose flour, cake flour, salt, and cinnamon into a medium bowl. Set aside.

Put the butter, sugar, and vanilla in the bowl of an electric mixer and beat on medium speed until smoothly blended, about 1 minute. Stop the mixer and scrape the sides of the bowl as needed. Reduce the speed to low, add the flour mixture, and mix just until incorporated.

Divide the dough into two equal parts. Put each on a large piece of plastic wrap and form into a log 5 in/12 cm long and 1½ in/4 cm in diameter. Roll each back and forth to form a smooth cylinder, then wrap in the plastic wrap. Refrigerate for at least 3 hours or overnight, until firm, or wrap aluminum foil over the plastic wrap and freeze for up to 2 months.

Frozen dough will be difficult to cut and should be defrosted in the refrigerator for at least 3 hours or overnight first.

When ready to bake the cookies, position a rack in the middle of the oven. Preheat the oven to 325°F/165°C/gas 3. Line two baking sheets with parchment paper. ***continued…***

SANDWICH COOKIES *with caramel filling & crunchy pecans* *(continued)*

Make the topping. In a small bowl, stir the pecans, maple syrup, and salt together until the pecans are evenly coated.

Use a large, sharp knife to cut each cold log into 27 slices about ³⁄₁₆ in/5 mm thick. Place the cookies 1½ in/4 cm apart on the baking sheets. Place a bit of the topping in the center of half of the cookies, using 3 or 4 pieces of chopped pecan per cookie, along with any syrup that clings to them. Gently press the pecans into the dough.

Bake the cookies one sheet at a time until they darken slightly, about 17 minutes.

Let cool on the baking sheet for 10 minutes. Use a wide metal spatula to transfer the cookies to a wire rack to cool completely.

Make the filling. Put the cream in a small saucepan and warm it over low heat. Don't let it boil. Adjust the heat to keep the cream warm while you cook the sugar.

Combine the sugar and water in a heavy saucepan with a capacity of at least 3 qt/3 L. Cover and cook over medium heat until the sugar dissolves, about 5 minutes. Uncover, increase the heat to medium-high, and bring the mixture to a boil. Boil until the mixture turns a dark golden color, tilting the pan slightly to ensure the sugar cooks evenly, about 10 minutes. Once the caramel begins to change color, it reaches the dark golden stage quickly, so watch it carefully and remove it from the heat immediately when it is ready.

Use a wooden spoon to slowly stir in the hot cream. The mixture will bubble up a lot, so be careful. Continue stirring slowly until the cream and caramel are evenly combined. Let cool until thick enough to cling to the cookies, at least 30 minutes. Alternatively, once the sauce has cooled for about 30 minutes, cover and refrigerate for up to 1 week. To use it, warm it over low heat just until soft enough to spread.

Turn the plain cookies (without the pecan topping) flat-side up. Spoon about 1 tsp caramel in the center of each. Top with the pecan-topped cookies, pecan-side up.

The cookies can be stored between layers of wax paper in a tightly covered container at room temperature for up to 3 days.

VANILLA *cookies with fudge filling*

There is no question that vanilla and chocolate are one of the all-time favorite flavor combinations. In this recipe, melt-in-your-mouth dark chocolate ganache is sandwiched between vanilla cookies and also used for decoration, making for an all-time favorite cookie choice. They look pretty on a cookie platter arranged with Pure Chocolate Sandwich Cookies (page 84), and the duo is a good choice for serving at parties.

MEASURING & MIXING TIME *10 minutes*

BAKE AT *350°F/180°C/gas 4* FOR ABOUT *20 minutes*

COOKIES

¾ cup/90 g unbleached all-purpose flour

6 tbsp/40 g cornstarch

¼ tsp baking powder

¼ tsp salt

½ cup/115 g unsalted butter, at room temperature

⅓ cup/65 g sugar

1 egg yolk

1 tsp vanilla extract

CHOCOLATE GANACHE

¼ cup/60 ml heavy cream

1 ½ tsp unsalted butter

3 oz/85 g semisweet chocolate, chopped

½ tsp vanilla extract

Make the cookies. Sift the flour, cornstarch, baking powder, and salt into a medium bowl. Set aside.

Put the butter and sugar in the bowl of an electric mixer and beat on medium speed until smoothly blended, about 1 minute. Stop the mixer and scrape the sides of the bowl as needed. Mix in the egg yolk and vanilla until blended, about 1 minute. Reduce the speed to low, add the flour mixture, and mix just until incorporated.

Divide the dough into two equal parts. Put each on a large piece of plastic wrap and form into a log 4½ in/11 cm long and 1 in/2.5 cm in diameter. Roll each back and forth to form a smooth cylinder, then wrap in the plastic wrap. Refrigerate for at least 3 hours or overnight, until firm, or wrap aluminum foil over the plastic wrap and freeze for up to 2 months.

Frozen dough will be difficult to cut and should be defrosted in the refrigerator for at least 3 hours or overnight first.

When ready to bake the cookies, position a rack in the middle of the oven. Preheat the oven to 350°F/180°C/gas 4. Line two baking sheets with parchment paper.

Use a large, sharp knife to cut each cold log into 22 slices about ³⁄₁₆ in/5 mm thick. Place the cookies 1½ in/4 cm apart on the baking sheets.

Bake the cookies one sheet at a time until the edges begin to brown lightly, about 20 minutes.

Let cool on the baking sheet for 10 minutes. Use a wide metal spatula to transfer the cookies to a wire rack to cool completely.

Make the ganache. Put the cream and butter in a small saucepan over low heat and cook, stirring occasionally, until the cream is hot and the butter melts. Don't let the mixture boil. Remove from the heat, add the chocolate, and let sit for about 30 seconds to soften the chocolate. Whisk just until the chocolate is melted and the ganache is smooth, about 20 seconds. Stir in the vanilla.

Immediately use a fork or small spoon to drizzle thin lines of ganache over the tops of half the cookies. Let the remaining ganache cool and thicken until firm enough to spread on the cookies, about 20 minutes.

Turn the cookies without the ganache drizzle flat-side up. Put 1 tsp of ganache in the center of each. Top with the remaining cookies, drizzle-side up. Gently press the top cookie to spread the ganache evenly.

Once the chocolate drizzle is firm, the cookies can be stored between layers of wax paper in a tightly covered container at room temperature for up to 3 days. If the kitchen temperature is warm, store them in the refrigerator to keep the chocolate firm.

CHOICES

These cookies can also be sandwiched with jam. Raspberry or strawberry jam would be a good choice.

PURE CHOCOLATE SANDWICH *cookies*

Would you like to have a surefire recipe to satisfy the most desperate chocolate craving? I bet you would. All you have to do is bake these dark chocolate cookies, fill them with a simple ganache, and drizzle additional ganache over them. Cookies ready; craving gone.

MEASURING & MIXING TIME *15 minutes*

BAKE AT *325°F/165°C/gas 3* FOR ABOUT *15 minutes*

COOKIES

1 ¾ cups/215 g unbleached all-purpose flour

⅓ cup/30 g unsweetened Dutch-process cocoa powder

¼ tsp salt

1 cup/225 g unsalted butter, at room temperature

½ cup/100 g granulated sugar

⅓ cup/35 g powdered sugar

2 egg yolks

1 tsp vanilla extract

CHOCOLATE GANACHE

½ cup/120 ml heavy cream

1 tbsp unsalted butter

6 oz/170 g semisweet chocolate, chopped

1 tsp vanilla extract

Make the cookies. Sift the flour, cocoa powder, and salt into a medium bowl. Set aside.

Put the butter, granulated sugar, and powdered sugar in the bowl of an electric mixer and beat on medium speed until smoothly blended, about 1 minute. Stop the mixer and scrape the sides of the bowl as needed. Reduce the speed to low and mix in the egg yolks and vanilla until blended, about 30 seconds. Add the flour mixture and mix just until incorporated.

Divide the dough into two equal parts. Put each on a large piece of plastic wrap and form into a roughly shaped log 6½ in/16.5 cm long and 1½ in/4 cm in diameter. Roll each back and forth to form a smooth cylinder, then wrap in the plastic wrap. Refrigerate for about 30 minutes, then roll each log again to form a more uniformly shaped cylinder. Refrigerate for at least 2½ hours or overnight, until firm, or wrap aluminum foil over the plastic wrap and freeze for up to 2 months.

Frozen dough will be difficult to cut and should be defrosted in the refrigerator for at least 3 hours or overnight first.

When ready to bake the cookies, position a rack in the middle of the oven. Preheat the oven to 325°F/165°C/gas 3. Line two or three baking sheets with parchment paper.

Use a large, sharp knife to cut each cold log into 34 slices about 3/16 in/5 mm thick. Place the cookies 2 in/5 cm apart on the baking sheets.

Bake the cookies one sheet at a time just until the tops change from shiny to dull and feel firm if touched lightly, about 15 minutes.

Let cool on the baking sheet for 10 minutes. Use a wide metal spatula to transfer the cookies to a wire rack to cool completely.

Make the ganache. Put the cream and butter in a medium saucepan over low heat and cook, stirring occasionally, until the cream is hot and the butter melts. Don't let the mixture boil. Remove from the heat, add the chocolate, and let sit for about 30 seconds to soften the chocolate. Whisk just until the chocolate is melted and the ganache is smooth, about 20 seconds. Stir in the vanilla.

Immediately use a fork or small spoon to drizzle thin lines of ganache over the tops of half the cookies. Let the remaining ganache cool and thicken until firm enough to spread on the cookies, about 20 minutes.

Turn the cookies without the ganache drizzle flat-side up. Put 2 tsp of ganache in the center of each. Top with the remaining cookies, drizzle-side up. Gently press the top cookie to spread the ganache evenly.

Once the chocolate drizzle is firm, the cookies can be stored between layers of wax paper in a tightly covered container at room temperature for up to 3 days. If the kitchen temperature is warm, store them in the refrigerator to keep the chocolate firm.

CHOICES

• *Rather than drizzling ganache over the top cookies, dust them with powdered sugar.*
• *Drizzle melted white chocolate over the top cookies instead of drizzling with ganache.*

GINGERBREAD SANDWICH COOKIES
& gingerbread kids

These are two-from-one-recipe cookies. The dough is formed into thick oval disks and sliced. A small cutter is used to cut out gingerbread kids from half of the slices. These small gingerbread cookies can be dusted with powdered sugar or decorated. After the large slices have baked, jam is spread on the plain cookies, and then the large cookies with the cutout are placed on top to make jam-filled cookie sandwiches.

MEASURING & MIXING TIME **15 minutes**

BAKE AT **325°F/165°C/gas 3** FOR ABOUT **19 minutes**

---

1 ½ cups/185 g unbleached all-purpose flour

½ tsp baking powder

¼ tsp baking soda

2 tsp ground ginger

½ tsp ground cinnamon

¼ tsp ground nutmeg

¼ tsp ground cloves

4 tbsp/55 g unsalted butter, cut into pieces

¼ cup/50 g firmly packed dark brown sugar

¼ cup/60 ml maple syrup

1 egg yolk

Granulated sugar or currants for decorating (optional)

¾ cup/240 g apricot jam

Powdered sugar for dusting

Sift the flour, baking powder, baking soda, ginger, cinnamon, nutmeg, and cloves into the bowl of an electric mixer. Set aside.

Put the butter, brown sugar, and maple syrup in a medium saucepan over low heat and cook, stirring often, until the butter and sugar melt. Increase the heat to medium-high and bring to a boil, then remove from the heat. Let cool for 10 to 15 minutes.

In a medium bowl, whisk the egg yolk to break it up. While whisking constantly, slowly pour the warm butter mixture over the egg yolk. Whisk until evenly blended. Make a well in the center of the flour mixture and pour in the warm butter mixture. Use a large spoon to stir just until a smooth dough forms and starts to come away from the sides of the bowl.

Divide the dough into two equal parts. Put each on a large piece of plastic wrap and form into a thick, oval-shaped disk 3½ in/9 cm long, 2 in/5 cm wide at the widest point, and 2½ in/6 cm thick. Wrap each in the plastic wrap. Refrigerate for at least 3 hours or overnight, until firm, or wrap aluminum foil over the plastic wrap and freeze for up to 2 months.

Frozen dough will be difficult to cut and should be defrosted in the refrigerator for at least 3 hours or overnight before it is sliced. ***continued…***

GINGERBREAD SANDWICH COOKIES *& gingerbread kids* (continued)

When ready to bake, position an oven rack in the middle of the oven. Preheat the oven to 325°F/165°C/gas 3. Line two or three baking sheets with parchment paper.

Unwrap one disk of dough and use a large, sharp knife and a sawing motion to cut 20 slices about ⅛ in/3 mm thick. Place the slices 1 in/2.5 cm apart on the prepared baking sheets. Repeat with the second piece of dough. Use a small gingerbread person cutter, 2 in/5 cm long, to cut out small cookies from the center of half of the cookies (placing the cutter diagonally on the cookie works well). Slide a metal spatula under those cookies to loosen them from the parchment paper. Remove the cutouts and place them 1 in/2.5 cm apart on a separate baking sheet. Sprinkle the cutouts with granulated sugar or decorate with currants, if desired.

Bake the large cookies one sheet at a time just until the tops feel firm if touched lightly and the edges begin to color slightly, about 19 minutes. Bake the sheet of gingerbread kids just until the tops feel firm if touched lightly and the edges begin to color slightly, about 10 minutes.

Let cool on the baking sheet for 10 minutes. Use a wide metal spatula to transfer the cookies to a wire rack to cool completely.

Turn the large, whole cookies flat-side up. Spread about 2 tsp of apricot jam over each. Lightly dust the tops of the cookies with the cutouts with powdered sugar, then place them sugar-side up on top of the jam.

The sandwich cookies can be stored between layers of wax paper in a tightly covered container at room temperature for up to 4 days. The gingerbread kids can be stored separately in a tightly covered container at room temperature for up to 4 days.

CHOICES

Fill each sandwich cookie with about 2 tsp of Chocolate Ganache (pages 82 and 84).

LINZER *sweethearts*

These cookies use a simple, clever method to produce a heart cutout on a cookie. After the dough is sliced, a small, heart-shaped cookie cutter is used to cut out a heart shape from half of the cookies, then all of the cookies, including the cutouts, are baked. After baking, the whole cookies are spread with red raspberry jam (strawberry works well too). Then the cookies with the cutouts are dusted with powdered sugar and placed on top of the jam. Voilà! Gorgeous sandwich cookie sweethearts—with the bonus of tiny, heart-shaped cookies to enjoy plain.

MEASURING & MIXING TIME *15 minutes*

BAKE AT *325°F/165°C/gas 3* FOR ABOUT *15 minutes*

2 cups/255 g unbleached all-purpose flour

½ tsp salt

1 cup/225 g unsalted butter, at room temperature

¾ cup/75 g powdered sugar, plus more for dusting

1 cup/145 g toasted almonds, ground

1 tsp vanilla extract

½ tsp almond extract

About 1 cup/320 g seedless raspberry jam

Sift the flour and salt into a medium bowl. Set aside.

Put the butter and powdered sugar in the bowl of an electric mixer and beat on medium speed until smoothly blended and the color lightens slightly, about 2 minutes. Stop the mixer and scrape the sides of the bowl as needed. Mix in the almonds, vanilla, and almond extract until blended, about 1 minute. Reduce the speed to low, add the flour mixture, and mix just until incorporated.

Divide the dough into two equal parts. Put each on a large piece of plastic wrap and form into a roughly shaped log 5½ in/14 cm long and 1¾ in/4.5 cm in diameter. Roll each back and forth to form a smooth cylinder, then wrap in the plastic wrap. Refrigerate for about 30 minutes, then roll each log again to form a more uniformly shaped cylinder. Refrigerate for at least 2½ hours or overnight, until firm, or wrap aluminum foil over the plastic wrap and freeze for up to 2 months.

Frozen dough will be difficult to cut and should be defrosted in the refrigerator for at least 3 hours or overnight first.

When ready to bake the cookies, position a rack in the middle of the oven. Preheat the oven to 325°F/165°C/gas 3. Line two or three baking sheets with parchment paper.

Use a large, sharp knife to cut each cold log into 22 slices about ¼ in/6 mm thick. Place the cookies 1 in/2.5 cm apart on the baking sheets. (These cookies don't spread much.) Use a small heart-shaped cutter, 1 in/2.5 cm long, to cut out hearts from the center of half of the cookies. Slide a metal spatula under those cookies to loosen them from the parchment paper. Remove the heart cutouts and place them ¾ in/ 2 cm apart on the baking sheets. *continued...*

LINZER *sweethearts (continued)*

Bake the cookies one sheet at a time until the edges begin to brown but the centers remain pale, about 15 minutes.

Let cool on the baking sheet for 10 minutes. Use a wide metal spatula to transfer the cookies to a wire rack to cool completely.

Turn the large, whole cookies flat-side up. Spread about 2 tsp of raspberry jam over each. Lightly dust the tops of the cookies with the cutouts with powdered sugar, then place them sugar-side up on top of the jam. Dust the small hearts with powdered sugar.

The sandwich cookies can be stored between layers of wax paper in a tightly covered container at room temperature for up to 3 days. The small hearts can be stored separately in a tightly covered container at room temperature for up to 3 days.

CHOCOLATE-DIPPED OATMEAL *cookie*
ice cream sandwiches

MAKES **18**

Prepare these ice cream sandwiches in advance and keep them in the freezer, ready to serve at a moment's notice. Crisp oatmeal cookies (delicious on their own) are half dipped in milk chocolate coating (making them even more delicious). Then ice cream is sandwiched between them (for ultimate deliciousness). Any flavor of ice cream, or even two flavors per sandwich, can be used. Good choices include vanilla, chocolate, coffee, dulce de leche, and raspberry. Once made into ice cream sandwiches, the crisp-all-the-way-through cookies will keep their good texture for up to two weeks in the freezer.

MEASURING & MIXING TIME **15 minutes**

BAKE AT **350°F/180°C/gas 4** FOR ABOUT **14 minutes**

COOKIES

1 cup/125 g unbleached all-purpose flour

½ tsp baking powder

½ tsp baking soda

½ tsp salt

¼ tsp ground cinnamon

½ cup/115 g unsalted butter, at room temperature

½ cup/100 g firmly packed light brown sugar

½ cup/100 g granulated sugar

1 egg

1 ½ tsp vanilla extract

1 ¼ cups/105 g old-fashioned rolled oats

1 cup/170 g milk chocolate chips

MILK CHOCOLATE COATING

12 oz/340 g milk chocolate, chopped

2 tbsp canola or corn oil

3 pints ice cream, softened until spreadable, but not melted

Make the cookies. Sift the flour, baking powder, baking soda, salt, and cinnamon into a medium bowl. Set aside.

Put the butter, brown sugar, and granulated sugar in the bowl of an electric mixer and beat on medium speed until smoothly blended, about 1 minute. Stop the mixer and scrape the sides of the bowl as needed. Mix in the egg and vanilla until blended, about 1 minute. Reduce the speed to low, add the flour mixture and oats, and mix just until incorporated. Add the chocolate chips and mix just until evenly distributed.

Divide the dough into two equal parts. Put each on a large piece of plastic wrap and pat into a rectangular slab 9 in/ 23 cm long, 4½ in/11 cm wide, and about ¾ in/2 cm thick. Wrap each in the plastic wrap. Refrigerate for at least 3 hours or overnight, until firm, or wrap aluminum foil over the plastic wrap and freeze for up to 2 months.

Frozen dough will be difficult to cut and should be defrosted in the refrigerator for at least 3 hours or overnight first.

When ready to bake the cookies, position a rack in the middle of the oven. Preheat the oven to 350°F/180°C/gas 4. Line two baking sheets with parchment paper.

Use a large, sharp knife to cut each slab into three rows lengthwise and six rows crosswise to form 18 pieces, each about 1½ in/4 cm square. Although the cookies are cut into squares, they will spread into rounds during baking. Place the cookies 2 in/5 cm apart on the baking sheets.

Bake the cookies one sheet at a time just until the edges and bottoms are lightly browned and the tops feel firm if touched lightly, about 14 minutes.

Let cool on the baking sheet for 10 minutes. Use a wide metal spatula to transfer the cookies to a wire rack to cool completely.

Make the coating. Put the chocolate and oil in a heatproof bowl or the top of a double boiler and place it over a saucepan of barely simmering water or the bottom of the double boiler; the water should not touch the bowl. Stir until the chocolate is melted and smooth. Scrape the mixture into a medium bowl and set aside for about 5 minutes to cool and thicken slightly.

Spread out a large piece of wax paper. Sweep the top of each cookie through the chocolate coating, covering about half of the top surface. Place the cookies on the wax paper and let sit until the chocolate coating is firm, about 1 hour at room temperature, or sooner if refrigerated. You will have a small quantity of chocolate coating left over for another use, but the larger quantity makes it easier to coat the cookies.

Wrap the cookies in plastic wrap individually and freeze them for at least 30 minutes or overnight. This prevents the ice cream from melting as the sandwiches are assembled.

Remove the cookies from the freezer and turn half of them flat-side up. Use an ice cream scoop or narrow metal spatula to spread about ⅓ cup of the ice cream over the flat bottom of one cookie. Top with another cookie, flat-side down, and with the chocolate coated half opposite the chocolate coated half on the bottom so every bite will have chocolate coating. Gently press the cookie onto the ice cream. Wrap tightly in plastic wrap (the original plastic wrap should work) and freeze. Continue filling and freezing the remaining cookies. Freeze for at least 5 hours or up to 2 weeks. For longer than overnight storage, seal the wrapped ice cream sandwiches in a clean, rigid container. Serve frozen.

CHOICES

- *Substitute semisweet chocolate chips or semisweet chocolate for the milk chocolate in either the dough or the coating.*
- *Add ½ cup/55 g of walnuts or pecans, coarsely chopped, to the dough when adding the chocolate chips.*
- *Press chopped nuts, colored sprinkles, or chocolate sprinkles onto the chocolate coating just after dipping the cookies, while the chocolate is still soft, or press them into the ice cream along the edges of the sandwiches.*

SAVORY COOKIES

Rather than sweet endings, think appetizing beginnings for these cookies. They are rich and flavorful, featuring cheese, herbs, olives, and even bacon and ham. All make excellent appetizers and are fine fare for cocktail parties. Two of them are similar to strudel; they are heartier and pair well with salads or soups.

The best types of cookie dough for transforming from sweet to savory are recipes that include little or no sugar. Cream cheese dough, sour cream pastry, and buttery dough are some of the options that are reliably easy to put together and work well with savory additions. Savory ingredients can be mixed into doughs, or they can be added to cookies after baking. And, as with sweet cookies, savory cookies can be stuffed before baking or sandwiched with different fillings after baking. The mouthwatering recipes in this chapter include cookies that have a ham and cheese filling baked inside; delicate wafers with fresh dill and Havarti incorporated into the dough; and simple cream crackers sandwiching a creamy filling that features lemon, garlic, basil, and smoked paprika.

LEMON, DILL & HAVARTI *wafers*

MAKES **64**

Lemon and dill are my go-to spring flavors, and I use both to flavor these buttery cheese wafers. I like to maximize the dill flavor by using both fresh dill and Havarti with dill, but plain Havarti will work.

MEASURING & MIXING TIME **10 minutes**

BAKE AT **350°F/180°C/gas 4** FOR ABOUT **15 minutes**

1 cup/125 g unbleached all-purpose flour

½ tsp salt

¼ tsp baking powder

4 oz/115 g Havarti cheese (preferably Havarti with dill), grated

½ cup/115 g unsalted butter, at room temperature

2 tbsp finely chopped fresh dill weed

1 tsp grated lemon zest

Sift the flour, salt, and baking powder into a medium bowl. Set aside.

Put the cheese and butter in the bowl of an electric mixer and beat on medium speed until smoothly blended, about 1 minute. Stop the mixer and scrape the sides of the bowl as needed. Add the dill and lemon zest and mix until well blended. Reduce the speed to low, add the flour mixture, and mix just until it is incorporated and a soft dough forms, about 1 minute.

Divide the dough into two equal parts. Put each on a large piece of plastic wrap and form into a log 8 in/20 cm long and 1 in/2.5 cm in diameter. Roll each back and forth to form a smooth cylinder, then wrap in the plastic wrap. Refrigerate for at least 3 hours or overnight, until firm, or wrap alumi-num foil over the plastic wrap and freeze for up to 2 months.

Frozen dough will be difficult to cut and should be defrosted in the refrigerator for at least 3 hours or overnight first.

When ready to bake the cookies, position a rack in the middle of the oven. Preheat the oven to 350°F/180°C/gas 4. Line two or three baking sheets with parchment paper.

Use a large, sharp knife to cut each cold log into 32 slices about ¼ in/6 mm thick. Place the cookies 1 in/2.5 cm apart on the baking sheets. (These cookies don't spread much.)

Bake the cookies one sheet at a time just until the edges and bottoms are lightly browned, about 15 minutes. When the cookies are almost done, a bit of butter will be bubbling at the edges.

Let cool on the baking sheet for 10 minutes. Use a wide metal spatula to transfer the cookies to a wire rack to cool completely.

The cookies can be stored between layers of wax paper in a tightly covered container at room temperature for up to 2 days.

CHIVE & BLACK PEPPER *logs*

I am often asked how I develop my recipe ideas. These cookies provide a good example. I wanted a buttery and simple dough for these savory cookies. After producing several hard, tough cookies, I came up with the idea of trying my butter and cream cheese rugelach dough. Although rugelach are sweet, their dough isn't. That proved to be the key to making these meltingly tender, savory cookies. They are an ideal nibble to serve at cocktail parties. Without their topping, these cookies can be stored for up to two days, but once topped, they must be served immediately.

MEASURING & MIXING TIME *15 minutes*

BAKE AT **350°F/180°C/gas 4** FOR ABOUT **20 minutes**

COOKIES

2 cups/255 g unbleached all-purpose flour

1 tbsp sugar

½ tsp salt

3 tbsp finely chopped chives

1 tsp freshly ground black pepper

12 oz/340 g cream cheese, at room temperature, cut into 12 pieces

¾ cup/170 g cold unsalted butter, cut into 24 pieces

¼ cup/60 ml sour cream

TOPPING

2 tbsp mayonnaise

6 tbsp/30 g finely chopped chives

Make the cookies. Put the flour, sugar, salt, chives, and black pepper into the bowl of an electric mixer and mix on low speed until combined, about 15 seconds. With the mixer running, add the cream cheese and butter and mix just until the dough holds together in large clumps, about 20 seconds. Stop the mixer and scrape the sides of the bowl as needed. Add the sour cream and mix just until it is incorporated and a soft dough forms, about 20 seconds. The dough will be sticky.

Divide the dough into two equal parts. Put each on a large piece of plastic wrap and form into a square log 7½ in/17 cm long and 1½ in/4 cm square at the ends. Wrap in the plastic wrap and rotate the wrapped dough, patting it on all four sides to form long, straight, even edges. Refrigerate for at least 3 hours or overnight, until firm, or wrap aluminum foil over the plastic wrap and freeze for up to 2 months.

Frozen dough will be difficult to cut and should be defrosted in the refrigerator for at least 3 hours or overnight first.

When ready to bake the cookies, position a rack in the middle of the oven. Preheat the oven to 350°F/180°C/gas 4. Line a baking sheet with parchment paper. ***continued…***

Each rectangular log will be sliced in three different directions to yield 18 narrow pieces 2½ in/6 cm long. First, use a large, sharp knife to cut the log into thirds crosswise to make 3 pieces, each 2½ in/6 cm long and 1½ in/4 cm square at the ends. Cut each in half lengthwise; you now have 6 pieces, each 2½ in/6 cm long, 1½ in/4 cm wide, and ¾ in/2 cm thick. Cut each of these in thirds; you now have 18 pieces 2½ in/6 cm long, ½ in/12 mm wide, and ¾ in/2 cm thick. Place the pieces 1 in/2.5 cm apart on the prepared baking sheets.

Bake the cookies until the bottoms are brown and the tops just begin to brown, about 20 minutes.

Let cool on the baking sheet for 10 minutes. Use a wide metal spatula to transfer the cookies to a wire rack to cool completely.

Before the topping is added, the cookies can be stored in a tightly covered container at room temperature for up to 2 days.

Add the topping. Spread a thin layer of the mayonnaise around the ends of each cookie, then dip each in the chopped chives to lightly coat. Arrange on a platter and serve immediately.

BLACK PEPPER & PARMESAN *crisps*

MAKES **64**

Forget the chips; instead, try these can't-eat-just-one crackers. A basket of these crisps can accompany antipasto, travel to a picnic, or simply be enjoyed as an afternoon snack.

MEASURING & MIXING TIME *10 minutes*

BAKE AT *450°F/230°C/gas 8* FOR ABOUT *11 minutes*

COOKIES

1 cup/125 g unbleached all-purpose flour

¼ tsp salt

1 cup/225 g cold unsalted butter, cut into 32 pieces

5 to 6 tbsp ice water

3 tbsp unsalted butter, melted

Salt for sprinkling

TOPPING

5 tbsp/50 g freshly grated Parmesan cheese

¾ tsp paprika

¾ tsp freshly ground black pepper

Make the cookies. Put the flour and salt in the bowl of an electric mixer and mix on low speed for several seconds to combine. Add the cold butter and mix just until it is in pieces the size of small lima beans, about 45 seconds. The butter pieces will be different sizes, and there will be some loose flour. With the mixer running, gradually add 5 tbsp of the water, 1 tbsp at a time. Stop mixing as soon as the mixture begins to hold together in large clumps, adding the remaining water 1 tsp at a time if necessary.

Gather the dough together and divide it into two equal parts. Transfer to a lightly floured surface. Working with one piece of dough at a time, use the heel of your hand to push the dough down and forward, then fold it in half. Repeat about six times to form a smooth dough.

Put each piece of dough on a large piece of plastic wrap and form into a log 6 in/15 cm long and 1½ in/4 cm in diameter. Roll each back and forth to form a smooth cylinder, then wrap in the plastic wrap. Refrigerate for at least 3 hours or overnight, until firm, or wrap aluminum foil over the plastic wrap and freeze for up to 2 months.

Frozen dough will be difficult to cut and should be defrosted in the refrigerator for at least 3 hours or overnight first.

When ready to bake the cookies, position a rack in the middle of the oven. Preheat the oven to 450°F/230°C/gas 8. Line two baking sheets with parchment paper.

Make the topping. In a small bowl, stir the cheese, paprika, and pepper together until well combined.

Use a large, sharp knife to cut each cold log into 32 slices about $3/16$ in/5 mm thick. Place the cookies 1 in/2.5 cm apart on the baking sheets. (These cookies don't spread much.) Use a pastry brush to lightly coat the cookies with the melted butter. Sprinkle a pinch of salt over each cookie. Sprinkle about ¼ tsp of the cheese mixture over each.

Bake the cookies one sheet at a time just until they become golden and the cheese melts, about 11 minutes.

Let cool on the baking sheet for 10 minutes. Use a wide metal spatula to transfer the cookies to a wire rack to cool completely.

The cookies can be stored in a tightly covered container at room temperature for up to 4 days.

BACON & CHEDDAR *crisps*

MAKES 32

Two ingredients, one obvious and one secretive, contribute to the crisp-all-the-way-through texture of these cookies. Bacon that's been cooked to a crisp is the obvious one, and crisp rice cereal is the elusive one. Although you won't see or taste the cereal, it makes for an unusual and appealing texture.

MEASURING & MIXING TIME *10 minutes*

BAKE AT *350°F/180°C/gas 4* FOR ABOUT *15 minutes*

4 oz/115 g sharp Cheddar cheese, grated

½ cup/115 g unsalted butter, at room temperature

4 oz/115 g crisp cooked bacon, crumbled

1 cup/125 g unbleached all-purpose flour

¼ tsp salt

½ tsp dry mustard

1 tsp Worcestershire sauce

¼ tsp hot pepper sauce (such as Tabasco)

1 cup/25 g crisp rice cereal

Put the cheese and butter in the bowl of an electric mixer and beat on medium speed until smoothly blended, about 1 minute. Stop the mixer and scrape the sides of the bowl as needed. Add the bacon and mix until evenly distributed. Reduce the speed to low, add the flour, salt, mustard, Worcestershire sauce, and hot pepper sauce, and mix just until evenly blended and a soft dough forms, about 1 minute. Add the cereal and mix just until evenly distributed.

Divide the dough into two equal parts. Put each on a large piece of plastic wrap and form into a log 8 in/20 cm long and 1 in/2.5 cm in diameter. Roll each back and forth to form a smooth cylinder, then wrap in the plastic wrap. Refrigerate for at least 3 hours or overnight, until firm, or wrap aluminum foil over the plastic wrap and freeze for up to 2 months.

Frozen dough will be difficult to cut and should be defrosted in the refrigerator for at least 3 hours or overnight first.

When ready to bake the cookies, position a rack in the middle of the oven. Preheat the oven to 350°F/180°C/gas 4. Line two baking sheets with parchment paper.

Use a large, sharp knife to cut each cold log into 16 slices about ½ in/12 mm thick. Place the cookies 2 in/5 cm apart on the baking sheets. Let sit for 10 minutes to soften slightly. Use the tines of a fork to press a crosshatch pattern on top of each cookie. The cookies should now be about ³/₁₆ in/5 mm thick.

Bake the cookies one sheet at a time just until the edges and bottoms are lightly browned, about 15 minutes.

Let cool on the baking sheet for 10 minutes. Use a wide metal spatula to transfer the cookies to a wire rack to cool completely.

The cookies can be stored in a tightly covered container at room temperature for up to 3 days.

HAZELNUT & BLUE CHEESE *thumbprints*

These savory thumbprint cookies are rolled in chopped hazelnuts, and the traditional jam center is replaced with a creamy blend of blue cheese and cream cheese.

MEASURING & MIXING TIME *10 minutes*

BAKE AT *325°F/165°C/gas 3* FOR ABOUT *22 minutes*

1 cup/125 g unbleached all-purpose flour

½ tsp salt

¼ tsp baking powder

½ cup/115 g unsalted butter, at room temperature

1 tbsp sugar

1 egg, separated

6 tbsp/40 g hazelnuts, skinned and toasted (see page 12),
 finely chopped

2 oz/55 g blue cheese, crumbled

2 oz/55 g cream cheese, at room temperature

Sift the flour, salt, and baking powder into a medium bowl. Set aside.

Put the butter and sugar in the bowl of an electric mixer and beat on medium speed until smoothly blended, about 30 seconds. Stop the mixer and scrape the sides of the bowl as needed. Mix in the egg yolk until blended, about 1 minute. Reduce the speed to low, add the flour mixture, and mix just until incorporated.

Divide the dough into two equal parts. Put each on a large piece of plastic wrap and form into a log 7 in/17 cm long and 1 in/2.5 cm in diameter. Roll each back and forth to form a smooth cylinder.

Use a fork to beat the egg white until foamy. Use a pastry brush to lightly coat each roll with the egg white. Sprinkle

half of the hazelnuts over each log and roll back and forth until evenly coated, gently pressing the hazelnuts into the dough. Wrap in the plastic wrap. Refrigerate for at least 3 hours or overnight, until firm, or wrap aluminum foil over the plastic wrap and freeze for up to 2 months.

Frozen dough will be difficult to cut and should be defrosted in the refrigerator for at least 3 hours or overnight first.

When ready to bake the cookies, position a rack in the middle of the oven. Preheat the oven to 325°F/165°C/gas 3. Line two baking sheets with parchment paper.

In a small bowl, stir the blue cheese and cream cheese together until smoothly blended.

Use a large, sharp knife to cut each cold log into 14 slices about ½ in/12 mm thick. Place the slices 1 in/2.5 cm apart on the baking sheets. (These cookies don't spread much.) Use a small spoon or your thumb to press an indentation, about ¼ in/6 mm deep, in the center of each cookie. Put about ¼ tsp of the blue cheese mixture in each indentation.

Bake the cookies one sheet at a time just until the edges and bottoms are browned and the cheese is evenly melted, about 22 minutes.

Let cool on the baking sheet for 10 minutes. Use a wide metal spatula to transfer the cookies to a wire rack to cool completely. Serve warm or at room temperature.

The cookies can be stored in a tightly covered container at room temperature for up to 2 days.

HAM & SWISS *swirls*

A crisp crust with melted cheese, mustard, and ham yields a fancy yet easy appetizer or accompaniment for salad or soup. Have the deli slice the meat and cheese thinly so they cling to the dough; you can roll the pastry tightly and the layers won't separate during baking.

MEASURING & MIXING TIME **15 minutes**

BAKE AT **350°F/180°C/gas 4** FOR ABOUT **22 minutes**

1 cup/125 g unbleached all-purpose flour
¼ tsp salt
6 tbsp/85 g unsalted butter, at room temperature
6 oz/170 g cream cheese, at room temperature
4 oz/115 g baked ham or black forest ham, thinly sliced
2 tbsp plus 2 tsp Dijon mustard
6 oz Swiss cheese, thinly sliced

Sift the flour and salt together into a medium bowl. Set aside.

Put the butter and cream cheese in the bowl of an electric mixer and mix on low speed until well blended. Stop the mixer and scrape the sides of the bowl as needed. Add the flour and mix until a smooth dough forms, about 1 minute.

Divide the dough into two equal parts. Put each on a large piece of plastic wrap and pat into about a square slab 5 in/12 cm across. Wrap each in the plastic wrap. Refrigerate for 1 hour or overnight. If dough is chilled for more than 3 hours, let it rest at room temperature for about 30 minutes so it will roll out easily.

Put one piece of cold dough on a lightly floured work surface and roll it out to a rectangle 10 in/25 cm long and 6 in/15 cm wide, with a long edge facing you. Leaving a bare edge ½ in/12 mm wide along the top long edge, arrange half of the ham over the dough, spread half of the mustard over the ham, and arrange half of the cheese over the mustard. The

ham and cheese should completely cover the dough except the ½ in/12 mm uncovered edge. Starting at the long edge facing you, roll the dough up into a tight log. Pinch the seam along the length of the roll to seal it tightly. Pinch the ends to seal them tightly. The log will be about 9 in/23 cm long. Slide the log onto a piece of plastic wrap and wrap tightly. Repeat to form a second log. Refrigerate for at least 2 hours or overnight, until firm, or wrap aluminum foil over the plastic wrap and freeze for up to 2 months.

Frozen dough will be difficult to cut and should be defrosted in the refrigerator for at least 3 hours or overnight first.

When ready to bake the cookies, position a rack in the middle of the oven. Preheat the oven to 350°F/180°C/gas 4. Line two baking sheets with parchment paper.

Use a large, sharp knife to cut each cold log into 18 slices about ½ in/12 mm thick. Place the cookies 1 in/2.5 cm apart on the baking sheets. (These cookies don't spread much.)

Bake the cookies one sheet at a time just until they are browned and the cheese is bubbling gently, about 22 minutes.

Let cool on the baking sheet for 10 minutes. The cookies can be served warm, or use a wide metal spatula to transfer them to a wire rack to cool completely.

The cookies can be stored between layers of wax paper in a tightly covered container at room temperature for up to 2 days. Warm them in an oven preheated to 275°F/135°C/gas 1 for about 10 minutes before serving.

FLAKY COOKIES
stuffed with cashews, carrot & chutney

I've been baking both sweet and savory recipes with this sour cream pastry for many years, but I'm still amazed every time I make it. Although it takes less than three minutes to mix the dough in an electric mixer, the result is so similar to a crisp, buttery, many-layered puff pastry. The filling, replete with carrot, fresh herbs, and chutney, has a nice kick from cayenne pepper and is the perfect counterpart to the buttery cookie.

MEASURING & MIXING TIME *15 minutes*

BAKE AT *375°F/190°C/gas 5* FOR ABOUT *15 minutes*

COOKIES
2 cups/255 g unbleached all-purpose flour

1 tsp baking soda

½ tsp salt

1 cup/225 g cold unsalted butter, cut into 32 pieces

½ cup/120 ml sour cream

FILLING
¼ cup/30 g finely grated carrot

¼ cup/30 g roasted cashews, coarsely chopped

3 tbsp mango chutney

2 tbsp finely chopped fresh mint

4 tsp finely chopped fresh cilantro

¾ tsp curry powder

¼ tsp ground cayenne pepper, or to taste

EGG WASH (optional)
1 egg

2 tbsp heavy cream

Make the cookies. Sift the flour, baking soda, and salt into the bowl of an electric mixer. Add the butter and mix on low speed until the butter is in pieces the size of small lima beans, about 1 minute. The butter pieces will be different sizes and there will be some loose flour. Add the sour cream and mix just until the dough holds together in large, smooth clumps that pull away from the sides of the bowl, about 30 seconds.

Divide the dough into two equal parts. Put each on a large piece of plastic wrap and form into a square log 5 in/12 cm long and 2 in/5 cm square at the ends. Wrap in the plastic wrap and rotate the wrapped dough, patting it on all four sides to form long, straight, even edges. Refrigerate for at least 3 hours or overnight, until firm, or wrap aluminum foil over the plastic wrap and freeze for up to 2 months.

Frozen dough will be difficult to cut and should be defrosted in the refrigerator for at least 3 hours or overnight first.

When ready to bake the cookies, position a rack in the middle of the oven. Preheat the oven to 375°F/190°C/gas 5. Line two baking sheets with parchment paper.

Make the filling. In a medium bowl, stir the carrot, cashews, chutney, mint, cilantro, curry powder, and cayenne together until well combined.

Use a large, sharp knife to cut each cold log into 20 slices about ¼ in/6 mm thick. Place half of the cookies 2 in/5 cm apart on the baking sheets. Put about 1 tsp of filling in the center of each. Top each with another cookie. Use the tines of a fork to press the edges together to seal them. The cookies may crack slightly on top. This is fine; the filling won't leak.

Make the egg wash, if desired. Whisk the egg and cream together until smooth and well blended. Use a pastry brush to lightly coat the top of each cookie with egg wash. This will add a light brown shine to the top of the cookies once they're baked.

Bake the cookies one sheet at a time until the tops feel firm if touched lightly and the edges begin to brown, about 15 minutes.

Let cool on the baking sheet for 10 minutes. Use a wide metal spatula to transfer the cookies to a wire rack to cool completely.

The cookies are best served the same day they are baked. However, they can be stored overnight in a tightly sealed container at room temperature. Warm them in an oven preheated to 250°F/120°C/gas ½ for about 10 minutes before serving.

WAFERS *stuffed with figs & tapenade*

Sweet and salty are some of our biggest cravings, and this is a recipe to satisfy both (see photo, page 94). Wafers made from a cream cheese dough are filled with sweet dried figs and salty olive tapenade. The filling can be quickly mixed in a mini food processor, which works much better than a standard-size food processor for the small quantity needed to fill the cookies.

MEASURING & MIXING TIME *15 minutes*

BAKE AT ***375°F/190°C/gas 5*** FOR ABOUT ***17 minutes***

PASTRY

1 cup/125 g unbleached all-purpose flour

1 tsp sugar

¼ tsp salt

6 tbsp/85 g unsalted butter, at room temperature

6 oz/170 g cream cheese, at room temperature

FILLING

2 ½ oz/70 g dried calimyrna figs (about 5 figs),
    stemmed and quartered

3 tbsp olive tapenade or black olive paste

1 tsp olive oil

¼ tsp grated orange zest

Olive oil for brushing
Freshly ground black pepper

Make the pastry. Sift the flour, sugar, and salt into a medium bowl. Set aside.

Put the butter and cream cheese in the bowl of an electric mixer and mix on low speed until well blended. Stop the mixer and scrape the sides of the bowl as needed. Add the flour and mix until a smooth dough forms, about 1 minute.

Divide the dough into two equal parts. Put each on a large piece of plastic wrap and form into a log 4 in/10 cm long and 1½ in/4 cm in diameter. Roll each back and forth to form a smooth cylinder, then wrap in the plastic wrap. Refrigerate for at least 3 hours or overnight, until firm, or wrap aluminum foil over the plastic wrap and freeze for up to 2 months.

Frozen dough will be difficult to cut and should be defrosted in the refrigerator for at least 3 hours or overnight first.

Make the filling. In a food processor, pulse the figs, tapenade, and olive oil until the figs are finely chopped and the mixture is combined. Transfer to a small bowl and stir in the orange zest. A mini food processor works well.

When ready to bake the cookies, position a rack in the middle of the oven. Preheat the oven to 375°F/190°C/gas 5. Line two baking sheets with parchment paper.

Use a small, sharp serrated knife and a sawing motion to cut each cold log into 32 slices about ⅛ in/3 mm thick. Place the cookies 1 in/2.5 cm apart on the baking sheets. (These cookies don't spread much.) Put about ½ tsp of filling in the center of each. Top each with another cookie. Use the tines of a fork to press the edges together to seal them. The cookies may crack slightly on top. This is fine; the filling won't leak. Use a pastry brush to lightly coat the top of each cookie with olive oil, then grind black pepper lightly over each.

Bake the cookies one sheet at a time just until the edges and bottoms are browned, about 17 minutes.

Let cool on the baking sheet for 10 minutes. Use a wide metal spatula to transfer the cookies to a wire rack to cool. Serve slightly warm or at room temperature.

The cookies can be stored in a tightly covered container at room temperature for up to 3 days.

SAVORY SANDWICH *cookies with creamy basil & smoked paprika filling*

*MAKES **28***

The thin cookies in this recipe have only four ingredients, which are quickly mixed in a food processor, and the filling, enhanced with the subtle flavor of smoked paprika, is similarly simple to put together. Any number of savory fillings could be sandwiched between these cookies, including store-bought fillings, to make preparation even easier. Fish or meat pâté or herb and garlic cream cheese would be good choices.

MEASURING & MIXING TIME *10 minutes*

BAKE AT *400°F/200°C/gas 6* FOR ABOUT *16 minutes*

COOKIES

1 cup/125 g unbleached all-purpose flour

½ tsp salt

4 tbsp/55 g cold unsalted butter, cut into 4 pieces

¼ cup/60 ml cold heavy cream

FILLING

6 oz/170 g cream cheese, at room temperature

3 tbsp finely chopped fresh basil, lightly packed

2 tbsp fresh lemon juice

1 garlic clove, minced

¾ tsp smoked paprika

¼ tsp salt

Smoked paprika for sprinkling

Make the cookies. In a food processor, pulse the flour, salt, and butter until the mixture looks crumbly. With the processor running, add the cream and process just until the mixture holds together. As soon as all of the cream is added, it will only take a couple of seconds for the dough to come together.

Divide the dough into two equal parts. Put each on a large piece of plastic wrap and form into a log 3½ in/9 cm long and 1½ in/4 cm in diameter. Roll each back and forth to form a smooth cylinder, then wrap in the plastic wrap. Refrigerate for at least 3 hours or overnight, until firm, or wrap aluminum foil over the plastic wrap and freeze for up to 2 months.

Frozen dough will be difficult to cut and should be defrosted in the refrigerator for at least 3 hours or overnight first.

When ready to bake the cookies, position a rack in the middle of the oven. Preheat the oven to 400°F/200°C/gas 6. Line two baking sheets with parchment paper.

Use a large, sharp knife to cut each cold log into 28 slices about ⅛ in/3 mm thick. Place the cookies 1 in/2.5 cm apart on the baking sheets. (These cookies don't spread much.)

Bake the cookies one sheet at a time just until the edges and bottoms are lightly browned, about 16 minutes.

Let cool on the baking sheet for 10 minutes. Use a wide metal spatula to transfer the cookies to a wire rack to cool completely.

Make the filling. In a medium bowl, stir the cream cheese, basil, lemon juice, garlic, paprika, and salt together until thoroughly blended.

Turn half of the cookies flat-side up and spread about 1 tsp of filling in the center of each. Top with the remaining cookies, flat-side down, and gently press to spread the filling. Lightly sprinkle with smoked paprika.

The cookies can be stored between layers of wax paper in a tightly covered container in the refrigerator for up to 3 days. Let sit at room temperature for about 15 minutes before serving.

ONION *strudel*

MAKES **24**

Strudel is more of a bake and slice, rather than a slice and bake, cookie, but I don't think anyone is going to quibble over that—certainly not when they bite into the crisp, buttery cream cheese pastry enclosing a filling of caramelized onions. Be sure to cool the cooked onions before spreading them over the dough. Warm onions would soften the dough and make it sticky and difficult to roll up. Since the strudel is sliced after baking, it can be baked straight from the freezer.

MEASURING & MIXING TIME *10 minutes*

BAKE AT *375°F/190°C/gas 5* FOR ABOUT *28 minutes*

PASTRY

1 cup/125 g unbleached all-purpose flour

1 tsp sugar

¼ tsp salt

6 tbsp/85 g unsalted butter, at room temperature

6 oz/170 g cream cheese, at room temperature

FILLING

2 tbsp unsalted butter

2 medium yellow onions, coarsely chopped

2 tbsp unsalted butter, melted

Freshly ground black pepper

Make the pastry. Sift the flour, sugar, and salt into a medium bowl. Set aside.

Put the butter and cream cheese in the bowl of an electric mixer and mix on low speed until well blended. Stop the mixer and scrape the sides of the bowl as needed. Add the flour mixture and mix until a smooth dough forms, about 1 minute.

Divide the dough into two equal parts. Put each on a large piece of plastic wrap and pat into a square slab 5 in/12 cm across. Wrap each in the plastic wrap. Refrigerate for 1 hour or overnight, until firm. If the dough is chilled for more than 3 hours, let it rest at room temperature for about 30 minutes so it will roll out easily.

Make the filling. In a frying pan, heat the butter over medium heat. Add the onions and cook, stirring occasionally, until the onions are very soft and browned at the edges, about 17 minutes.

Set aside to cool. The onions can be stored in a covered container in the refrigerator overnight.

Put one piece of dough on a lightly floured work surface and roll it out to a rectangle 10 in/25 cm long and 6 in/15 cm wide, with a long edge facing you. Lightly brush the dough with some of the melted butter. Leaving a bare edge ½ in/ 12 mm wide along the top long edge, spread half of the onions over the dough. Starting with the long edge facing you, roll the dough up into a tight log. Pinch the seam along the length of the roll to seal it tightly. Pinch the ends to seal them tightly. Brush with some of the melted butter and grind black pepper lightly over the top. Slide the log onto a piece of plastic wrap and wrap tightly. Repeat to form a second log.

Refrigerate for at least 2 hours or overnight, until firm, or wrap aluminum foil over the plastic wrap and freeze for up to 2 months. Frozen strudel does not need to be defrosted before baking.

When ready to bake the strudels, position a rack in the middle of the oven. Preheat the oven to 375°F/190°C/gas 5. Line a baking sheet with parchment paper.

Place the strudels 3 in/7.5 cm apart and seam-side down on the baking sheet.

Bake until lightly browned on top and browned on the bottom, about 28 minutes, or if using frozen strudel, about 32 minutes. The baked strudel will be about 12 in/30.5 cm long.

Let cool on the baking sheet for 10 minutes.

Use a large, sharp knife to cut the strudel into 1-in/2.5-cm slices. Serve warm.

The baked slices can be stored between layers of wax paper in a tightly covered container in the refrigerator for up to 2 days. Warm them in an oven preheated to 275°F/135°C/ gas 1 for about 10 minutes before serving.

SUN-DRIED TOMATO & BASIL *strudel*

MAKES **24**

These are the fastest savory slice and bake cookies on the block. The pastry is store-bought phyllo dough, and the filling is made in just a few minutes in a food processor. They are festive and hearty hors d'oeuvres, and their golden orange color flecked with green chives brightens any table.

Since phyllo pastry contains only flour and water, it acts the same way a flour and water paste does if allowed to dry out—it gets hard. The simple solution is to keep the unused stack of phyllo pastry covered with plastic wrap and a clean, damp dish towel as you work. If kept covered, the sheets of phyllo remain soft, pliable, and a pleasure to use. You'll find phyllo pastry in the freezer section near the piecrusts. One last tip: Defrosting the phyllo in its packaging in the refrigerator overnight before using it will help ensure that the sheets don't stick together.

MEASURING & PREPARATION TIME *10 minutes*

BAKE AT *375°F/190°C/gas 5* FOR ABOUT *30 minutes*

---

4 tbsp/55 g unsalted butter

2 tbsp olive oil

5 oil-packed sun-dried tomatoes, drained and coarsely chopped

1 large garlic clove, coarsely chopped

15 large basil leaves

1 egg

1 tbsp unbleached all-purpose flour

¼ tsp salt

¼ tsp freshly ground black pepper

8 oz/255 g cream cheese, at room temperature

¼ cup/60 ml sour cream

12 sheets phyllo dough, 12 in/30.5 cm long and 8 in/20 cm wide

In a small frying pan, heat the butter and olive oil over medium heat, stirring constantly until the butter melts. Remove from the heat and set aside.

In a food processor, pulse the tomatoes, garlic, and basil until finely chopped. Add the egg, flour, salt, and pepper and process just until the egg is blended into the mixture. Add the cream cheese and sour cream and process until smooth. Scrape into a bowl.

Put the stack of phyllo sheets on a work surface and cover with plastic wrap and a clean, damp dish towel. Place one phyllo sheet on a work surface with a long side facing you. Use a pastry brush to lightly coat the phyllo with the butter mixture. Repeat with two more sheets, then top with a fourth sheet. Leaving a bare edge 1 in/2.5 cm wide along the bottom and sides of the phyllo, spoon one-third of the cream cheese mixture in a strip 1½ in/4 cm wide along the bottom edge of the phyllo. Fold the sides of the phyllo in to enclose the edges of the filling, then roll the strudel up tightly. Lightly brush the top with the butter mixture. Repeat with the remaining phyllo and cream cheese mixture to make two more strudels. ***continued...***

SUN-DRIED TOMATO & BASIL *strudel (continued)*

The strudels are ready to bake, or wrap them in plastic wrap and then aluminum foil and freeze for up to 2 months. Frozen strudel does not need to be defrosted before baking.

When ready to bake the strudels, position a rack in the middle of the oven. Preheat the oven to 375°F/190°C/gas 5. Line a baking sheet with parchment paper.

Place the strudels 2 in/5 cm apart and seam-side down on the baking sheet. Use a sharp knife to score the top of the strudel at 1-in/2.5-cm intervals, cutting through the pastry but not into the filling. This makes it easier to slice the baked strudel.

Bake until golden on top, about 30 minutes, or if using frozen strudel, about 35 minutes.

Let cool on the baking sheet for 10 minutes. Use a wide metal spatula to transfer the strudels to a wire rack to cool completely. Use a sharp knife to cut each strudel into pieces where scored. Serve warm.

If serving the strudels at a party, bake one at a time for a continuous supply of warm strudel, or cover baked strudel loosely with aluminum foil and keep it warm for up to 1 hour in an oven preheated to 225°F/110°C/gas ¼.

CHOICES

Vary the ingredients and seasonings in the cream cheese filling; for example, season the cream cheese with basil, lemon zest, and garlic, or substitute chopped and sautéed onion, using 1 large onion, instead of the sun-dried tomatoes. Basically, you can use any combination of herbs and vegetables that is appealing.

INDEX